BLACK HORIZONS

One aviator's experience in the Post-Tuskegee Era

To: Russ

08/28/08

U. L. 'Rip' Gooch

with Glen Sharp

BLACK HORIZONS

Aviation Business Consultants
U. L. "Rip" Gooch
12 Crestview Lakes Estates
Wichita, Kansas 67220

Library of Congress Control Number: 2006937893
ISBN Number: 0-9786762-0-3

Graphic Design & Book layout by Larry G. Nichols II
Printed in the U.S.A. by Mennonite Press, Inc. Newton, KS
        First Printing, July 2006, Hardcover
        Second Printing, November 2006, Softcover

To Augusta, my wife of forty-nine years, who traveled with me from the fields of Tennessee to the state capital of Kansas. She led me, walked beside me and actively supported me in all my endeavors.

Also to Kerry, my son, a shining light that was dimmed too soon.

I miss them both immensely.

Table of Contents

About the Authors

(From right) Rip Gooch with his wife Augusta, son Kerry, granddaughter Dorian, and daughters Camille and Bonita at Kerry's college graduation, 1989.

In the immediate wake of the Tuskegee Airmen winning the right for blacks to fly combat missions during World War II, African American pilots were supposed to have entered an era of opportunity—but racism prevented it.

At a time when few black aviators worked professionally, U.L. "Rip" Gooch used sheer determination to build his own million-dollar airport operation in one of the most conservative states in the nation.

The son of rural Tennessee share-croppers and the grandson of emancipated slaves, Rip Gooch was orphaned at age four and fended for himself growing up in the 1920s and '30s under the shadow of Jim Crow. Working in fields while watching airplanes fly overhead, he dreamed of escaping to a better life.

Despite earning his wings on the GI Bill after World War II, Rip couldn't find full-time aviation work because he was black. After battling racism as an inspector with Boeing Airplane Co. in the 1950s, he decided to start his own flight business, which provided a stepping stone for a number of other black pilots. His work would eventually earn him a place in the Black Aviation Hall of Fame.

As years passed, Rip continued to break racial barriers by helping establish one of the first minority-owned banks in Kansas and becoming one of the few African-American to serve on the Wichita city council and the Kansas Senate.

• •

U.L. "Rip" Gooch is a pilot with 20,000 flight hours, a retired FAA pilot examiner and retired Kansas state senator, among other careers. A member of the Black Aviation Hall of Fame, he currently lives in Wichita, Kansas.

Glen Sharp is a Wichita-based freelance journalist who has served as a correspondent for The New York Times and Newsweek.

Preface

I was born on a large West Tennessee farm in 1923, the grandson of freed slaves and the son of field hands. As a black man aging over an eight decade period, I have observed life from a number of vantages, from last-class citizen in a nation blanketed in racial bigotry to respected member of society in a nation still filled with racial tension. This book chronicles how I confronted those economic and cultural barriers to rise from being a poor orphan to become an aircraft pilot, the owner of a million-dollar business and later a politician.

My grandparents' social position as freed slaves did not give them the opportunity to provide for their children as they would have liked, but what they had they gave. They knew their descendants would find it difficult to survive and would need to live with a substantial amount of humility and a stubborn will to persevere. As the United States progressed through the era of Civil Rights and toward a diversified society, my grandparents' judgment has remained apt.

As a child I never heard any of the older generations explain how to survive; it was simply regarded as a fact of life. Lessons were transmitted through laughter, story and song - a method that allowed us to accept reality without being spiritually wounded. I remember the story of Old Can't and Old Couldn't, two slaves running away from their masters. They were caught and Old Can't was beaten to death in front of Old Couldn't. Old Couldn't was then also beaten, but he survived and decided that he could after all. There was a lot of laughter in the telling of that story, but even the youngest among us understood the message: Don't ever say you can't do something. This story became the cornerstone of my philosophy in life, and helped me find the personal strength to move worlds away from my beginnings as an orphaned son of farm workers.

Many doors were closed to the children, grandchildren and great-grand-children of slaves because of the color of our skin. I have had the experience of trying to enter a number of those doors, never invited in by ringing the bell or knocking. Entrance was granted only after I kicked down those barriers. Whether my doors or the doors of others stay open is now up to a generation of African-Americans ignorant of the struggles of their forbears, a generation with a significant number of its members living in slums or prisons or depending on welfare, victims of our nation's culture. Perhaps they, too, could learn from the story of Old Couldn't.

Chapter 1
At the Bottom

Picture a Saturday morning street scene in the black section of a rural Tennessee town circa 1930. Families of area sharecroppers and farm hands come to shop for groceries and supplies, as well as to socialize during a respite from toiling in fields. While wives fantasize over new fabrics in the mercantile, some of their husbands amble toward the primitive hardware aisle or even slink out into the alley for a roll of dice.

The children play in groups along and in the dirt street where the black-owned and black-serving businesses are situated. In a setting where they rarely attend school past the eighth grade, if even to that point, and where it's figured they'll work in fields or at other menial jobs for their livings, "success" is a foreign word. Economic hardship (Great Depression or not) and racism dictate what paths they will take.

For all but three of the children in one particular play group, life would likely run its abused course within miles of Henning or maybe as far away as Memphis or Nashville. For these three exceptions, life would lead to confrontation, political involvement, distant travel and, on occasion, success.

Two of the three were brothers who already stood apart from the sharecroppers' offspring. Alex and George Haley's grandfather owned a local lumber mill, and their father had two college degrees. Alex (1921-92) grew up to be the author of the best-selling *Roots* and *The Autobiography of Malcolm X*. George (born 1926) became a lawyer and held a number of political posts before President Bill Clinton named him U.S. ambassador to Gambia in 1998.

I was the third exception, and aviation would become my ticket out of that world. At the time I first knew the Haley brothers nothing in my life would have indicated that I'd turn out any differently than the other children who played with us. All my grandparents were born into slavery, and all of them and their offspring struggled to survive. Though I didn't care much when I was young, for some reason I later developed a great desire to know my grandparents. I wanted to know their names and how they lived their lives. My desire to know more about them was like looking for the missing pieces of myself.

Knowing more about my family, who had been slaves in Tennessee and elsewhere, would give me a better sense of those who made my life possible. It would also erase a painful curiosity I could never completely explain or understand. I searched public records for years looking for any information, and asked everyone and anyone I thought may have known or possessed any information about the Gooches or my mother's family, the Harts.

In searching records and asking questions I did not locate the information I would have liked to find for myself and for my children. Oral history was not reliable. People were remembered by pet names or nicknames rather than their real names. Many people sincerely wanted to help me, but their memories did not serve them well. In courthouse records, the names of slaves or freed slaves could be found listed as the property of their owners or former owners, if you knew the correct spelling of their names. What I did find enriched me with a sense of pride for who my grandparents and predecessors had been and for what they had tried to become in spite of their limited circumstances.

My father's parents, Sam Thomas Gooch (born in 1855) and Frances Morrow Gooch (born in 1858), were both from North Carolina and migrated to Tennessee.

My grandmother, Frances Morrow Gooch, who was born in 1858. Her husband owned a hauling business and farm, but died prematurely, and the family never regained any measure of prosperity.

They may have known each other in North Carolina, but this can't be verified. They were married April 13, 1875, in Haywood County, Tennessee, and became the parents of seven children, the youngest of whom was my father, Frank Gooch. One of the girls was my Aunt Lula, who in my lifetime would become more to me than just my father's sister.

Sam Thomas Gooch was mulatto, having both black and white ancestry, a common occurrence during slavery. My grandfather can be traced to the farm of a man named Daniel Gooch in the town of Oak Hill in Granville County, North Carolina. A recent search of census records shows that in 1850 Daniel Gooch owned one female slave, aged 22, and three male slaves, aged 19, 24 and 52. The records also indicate that mulatto children were born to the household: Jeff in 1854, Samuel Thomas in 1855 and Prince in 1857 (he also ended up in Tennessee). The fact that these children are listed as mulatto rather than Negro points to Daniel Gooch having fathered them.

Eight years old at the time the slaves were emancipated, Sam Thomas Gooch would have reached manhood with his mixed heritage likely giving him the advantage of being able to kick down a few doors, or at least knock on some of them. Sam owned a hauling business, with mules and a wagon, and initiated the purchase of a farm. This seems to indicate that he was a man of courage and character, but before he realized his full potential, he was killed. During one hauling job in the 1890s he was crushed by a bale of cotton. His death as a fairly young man seems to have ended the prosperity of his family and their hopes for a life with fewer hardships as freed slaves. Neither the farm nor the hauling business that had been a part of the Gooches' life while Sam lived remained with his widow and children for more than a few years after his death.

My mother's family has been more difficult to trace, partly because I am not sure of the correct spelling of the name, which makes information hard to trace and unreliable. From the best information I could find, my mother's father was Lee Hart, her mother Ella T. Hart and Ella's father Palmer Loveless. I never knew Palmer Loveless, but I knew Lee Hart, though not in a traditional grand-father-grandson relationship. He was a vendor that I saw passing through the countryside selling fish out of a tin tub in the back of a truck. He knew that I was his daughter's son, but he never tried to have a conversation with me. When Mr. Hart passed where I lived he always left a catfish. "This is for the boy," he would say. Catfish have fewer bones than other fish, and it was safer for children to eat. For people who had to struggle to keep their stomachs filled, fish was a staple that we depended upon, and to this day it is my food of choice. My grandfather, in his way, showed his concern for me. As I have become a

The road leading to the Scott farm, where I was born, in rural Lauderdale County, Tennessee.

The two-room shack where I was born in 1923, one of several such structures on the lawn of the Scott family farm's big house in rural Lauderdale County, Tennessee.

grandfather I have derived a great deal of satisfaction from building bonds with my children and their children in an openly affectionate way that I never knew was possible in my early years. This true familial relationship has also allowed me to reflect upon my life in a manner that puts it in a perspective my offspring can identify with and appreciate; I make sure they know where they came from.

My mother and father, Mary Hart and Frank Gooch, met around 1920 on a Tennessee farm owned by a family named Scott. The Scott farm was a large, prosperous affair that employed many people for the variety of work that had to be done to run so large an operation. My mother and her daughter Christine, a ten-year-old from a previous relationship, both worked as house servants. My father was a farmhand. A great many things about the relationship between my parents is unknown, but they did produce a son. I was born on September 13, 1923, in a two-room shack near the Scott family home, the big house. Our shack was one of a row of such structures on the Scotts'

My mother, Mary Hart, in a detail from the only known photograph of her. She died when I was four.

lawn, and ours was the closest to the big house because my mother and sister worked inside.

As for my first and middle names, Ulysses Lee, I was told they were given to me by a member of the Scott family – and this turned out to be one of the worst things to happen to me. The illiterate farm folk, my parents included, couldn't pronounce Ulysses, nor could anyone at school. Part of it was ignorance, and part of it was the Southern dialect; even I couldn't pronounce it because I had a speech problem. People would say "Use," "Usey," "Uly" and other variations. Even my eighth grade graduation certificate is inscribed to "Ulys." I eventually started telling people I was named for the two commanding generals of the Civil War, Ulysses S. Grant of the Union and Robert E. Lee of the Confederacy, because my parents didn't want to show prejudice. Later, when I served in the military, people started referring to me as "Ripley" because I was from Ripley, Tennessee, and then that was shortened to "Rip."

I was told that my mother's name was Mary Gooch and that she and my father were married. The 1920 census record disputes this with a line drawn through the "Gooch" part of her name. Sometime after my birth, my father was dismissed from the Scott farm for unknown reasons. After his departure my mother remained on the farm until she became ill, when I was about four years old. My sister Christine went to live with a great aunt in Memphis. My mother and I went to live with her uncle, Frank Loveless, in a section of Lauderdale County, Tennessee, on the east side of the Mississippi River - an area called the Bottom because of its lack of elevation. Flooding was so common there that residents who couldn't afford to live elsewhere built their lodgings several feet above ground for protection. The people who lived or worked in the vicinity were stigmatized as being "from the Bottom."

O.W. Loveless, the son of my great uncle and my only surviving relative from my mother's family.

My mother died in the Bottom in the home of my great uncle. Though I have little real memory of my mother, and am unable to visualize her face, I believe I was near her as she died. Some people have told me I likely was not there and have just convinced myself otherwise, but I vividly recall being shooed from the room by some women who were to prepare her for the wake. My mother kept me with her as long as she could for reasons only a parent would truly understand. Dreams, memories and experiences can stay throughout a lifetime, but some stand apart from all others. Standing in the presence of my mother in the last moments of her life, and on through the preparation for her burial while she lay on an ironing board held by four old cane-bottom chairs is still fresh in my mind. I was only four years old at that time; after 80 years of replaying the scene in my head, I'm convinced I witnessed my mother's passage from this life.

The word "bottom" implies that one cannot go any lower. At this time in my life, that word described where and how I was living, as well as how I felt. The only place left for me to go was up.

Chapter 2
A New Home

Sometime following my mother's funeral, my estranged father rode up to my great uncle's home on a horse and took me from the people I knew to live with his sister, Lula, and her husband, Fred Reed. My father, who had probably never owned a horse, borrowed the animal from his sister, Daisy Watkins, who lived halfway between the Reed home on the east edge of Lauderdale County and where I had been staying in the Bottom, on the west end of the county. By horseback it was a long ride. My father and I stayed for an evening with Aunt Daisy and her husband and then proceeded to Lula and Fred's farm.

My father, who had never played a real role in my life up to that time, stayed with me one night and left the next day, leaving me with people I had never seen before. It was about a year before I saw him again, and on that occasion he took me into the woods where he worked as a tree cutter. I remember marveling at how the workers loaded logs onto extra-large wagons. They hooked what seemed like an enormous log to oxen that would drag it from the forest to the road, position the log parallel to the back of the log wagon, wrap a chain around the log and attach the other end to an ox at the front of the wagon. The ox would pull the log onto the wagon. Later, when I was in high school, I took a logging job for two weeks that required me to use a cable to attach logs to Caterpillar tractors (which had replaced the oxen) that would pull them through the forest while I used a large piece of wood to make the logs move in the right direction to avoid obstacles. For my back-breaking labor, I received about $1.50 a day.

I had left the Bottom with all that I owned stuffed into a paper sack; nothing of my mother's was given to me. I have often wished that I had something of hers I could cherish, but I have only memories.

One is a vague recollection of riding on a white horse with her in the Labor Day parade and picnic in Ripley, an annual, predominantly black homecoming-style event that attracts thousands of people from the county and beyond. Even people who've moved far from their beginnings in Lauderdale County return for the celebration. My mother likely took great pride in participating in the parade, riding among the fancily decorated floats made by local churches and other organizations. When the parade ended on the outskirts of town the celebrants would gather in a nearby cow pasture. The picnic didn't involve unpacking lunch and eating. It was a fair with open barbecue pits, giant black pots of fried fish, games and maybe a ride such as a Ferris wheel, though everyone had to watch not to step in cow pies. A baseball diamond would be laid out for local pick-up teams to compete, and people would socialize and watch the game. Years later, a prominent local white family named Rice donated land to the black community for a city park of their own where the picnic could be held. Entertainer Tina Turner, who grew up in a nearby burg, had memories of the Labor Day picnic fond enough to mention it in one of her songs, "Nutbush City Limits."

The Labor Day celebration is still an important facet of life there today, though it has grown immensely. A band of maybe eight or ten amateur musicians used to lead the parade, but the bands today consist of students from area high schools and may number more than a few hundred members. Additionally, most floats were pulled by horses decades ago, with the exception of perhaps a car or two. Today, hundreds of vehicles are involved, from three-wheelers and motorcycles to tractors and semi-trucks, but a few horses still are used in the parade and are admired much more now because they are no longer a common sight. The festivities, though, have remained a mostly black affair.

I also have a vivid memory of going with my mother to a tall, two-story building and staring up at a man looking down from behind barred windows. The man behind the bars was my father and the building was the Lauderdale County jail in Ripley. Though his behavior had never been anything but shiftless during my youth, the only bad thing I ever heard about him was that he drank too much; when I knew of him going to jail, it was for public drunkenness (he had been a pre-teen alcoholic). I take pride in that of all I've found about my mother, no unkind word has ever been spoken or written about her.

In contrast to my memories of my parents, I would always remember my life with Aunt Lula and Uncle Fred, who were sharecroppers. It did not take long for me to realize that Aunt Lula loved me. My uneasiness at being with strangers was soon replaced by feelings of being wanted and loved securely. I was the only child Aunt Lula would ever have; she would be the only mother I would ever really know. We were bonded by circumstances that gave each of us the love we both hoped for and needed.

In her late thirties, she, like my father, had a light complexion, resembling her father, who was mulatto. Of average height, she was not a petite woman and did not hesitate to engage in physical work on the farm. Raised to go to church, Aunt Lula clung to the tradition and was also a likable, kind and giving person, respected in the community. She also worked as a practical nurse, taking care of sick people who sometimes couldn't pay.

In his early forties, Uncle Fred was dark-skinned and obviously of African descent. He had a strong work ethic, was private, straightforward and honest.

He was not terribly generous because he believed people were responsible for their own misfortunes because they didn't work hard enough. He gave people respect and demanded it in return, never engaging in practical jokes or similar behavior. "Act like a man, you'll be treated like one," he told me. Fred thought education was a great asset and should be attained at any cost. If class was in session, he'd push me to attend rather than skip school and help with farm work. Had the Depression not happened, he could have elevated himself beyond the life of a sharecropper.

Uncle Fred, shown here in the 1950s, taught me the value of a strong work ethic, and didn't suffer foolishness from anyone.

When Aunt Lula took me to school to be enrolled for the first time my life began to expand. I was with strangers again in a strange place, but I didn't feel alone. The school was miles from our house, a long way for a little boy to walk, but after days of walking it did not seem so long. I quickly became acquainted with the other kids at school, some of whom walked each day with me.

The rural school was a two-level wooden building built by money from the Julius Rosenwald Foundation, a charitable organization formed by the president of Sears, Roebuck and Co. to fund construction of Negro schools throughout the South. The building may have been drafty, but it was of

Aunt Lula, who raised me, in her later years when she and uncle Fred were no longer farming.

higher quality than most colored schools in rural areas. Negro children did not have access to warm buildings like white children often did. We had to make do with whatever was available to us. In the rooms that we had, there were potbelly stoves that never quite cured the effects of wintertime. We knew about the cold weather. Some of our homes were more cold and drafty than the school. What was important was that as Negro children we were in a schoolhouse, period. The school had two teachers and they were very pleasant, which offset our hardships. When I came home from school, my aunt saw to it that I had companionship. She gave me a cat named Tom and a box of ABC blocks. Aunt Lula never failed to do her best to make me feel loved.

For those living in the country, childhood didn't last long. About the time children went to school they also went to the field to work, dragging their small sacks of cotton alongside those dragging long full sacks. In Tennessee cotton and corn were the money crops. Whole families labored because every hand was needed to plant and later harvest. Children learned early how to make a living. I was no different.

Life wasn't all work for sharecroppers. On most Saturdays, people went to the nearest town, Ripley, to visit or shop, and just feel relief from the routine of work. For the grown-ups who went to party, there was "the Hole," a section of town dedicated to drinking, gambling, playing music, dancing, and meeting others who thought life was too hard not to have a little fun. Children, as a rule, stayed home on Saturdays and played with other children whose parents had gone to town. Baseball, marbles and whatever crossed their minds kept them busy. We all knew about the Hole and what went on in town on Saturdays. When I was allowed to go to town I enjoyed it, but it was usually for a purpose and we would always return home by evening.

Late at night, when the reveling became too lively in the Hole, the sheriff would come through and blow a whistle, and both the out-of-towners and the locals had to head home, whether they were causing a ruckus or not.

Some of the events I particularly remember were those that involved my father. I remember several times seeing him drunk or in jail, which was always embarrassing for me. On one of those embarrassing Saturdays, I learned from him that I had a half-sister he called Puddin', and he tried to introduce us. Her relationship with him didn't appear to be any better than mine. What likely occurred was that she happened to be in town with her mother and Frank ran into them and soon after ran into me. "I'm takin' you to meet your sister," he slurred. I thought he meant my half-sister Christine, who was living in Memphis but would visit occasionally. He led me down the sidewalk to Puddin' and neither she nor I knew what to think. The two of us never met again following that awkward start. By the time I came to regret not getting to know Puddin', about fifty years had passed and my father died without telling me anything about her. Through various sources I found that she had also died. Though I never discovered her real name, I did learn she had a son named Johnny Frank Rice, who supposedly ended up in Memphis. My efforts to find him have proved unsuccessful.

My father and I had a relationship neither of us could just walk away from. Though constantly embarrassed with the way Frank Gooch acted, I had to respect him as my father. Likewise, he respected me as his son despite not knowing me as well as a father should. It would be a long time before I would understand that he could love me as a parent and still not be able to control himself as a man.

My father, Frank Gooch, with me in around 1941. He was a pre-teen alcoholic, but quit drinking cold turkey several years after this photo was taken.

—Reflections—

My eighth-grade diploma. Note that my first name is spelled "Ulys" because people could neither pronounce nor write "Ulysses."

Chapter 3
Aim High

For some, Sunday was just a continuation of Saturday, but for others it was the Lord's Day. Churches were a good distance from where most of us lived. Getting ready to go to church was much like getting ready to go to town. People would probably be gone for most of the day. There were many in our community who possessed missionary minds about Sunday. Playing baseball and other "sinful" amusements were considered disrespectful and shameful. Those of us who didn't treat the Lord's Day accordingly were told that God had his eyes on us. I am sure the church folk knew about the death of my mother and the condition of my father and saw me as an outreach project for their ministry.

One such person was my aunt and uncle's neighbor, Mrs. Alberta Picket. She was a Baptist Sunday school teacher who saw that I wasn't keeping the Sabbath in a way she thought appropriate. Mrs. Picket decided I'd be well served to attend Sunday school, even though I'd often attend the actual church service with Aunt Lula. My aunt agreed that it would be good for me to be in Sunday school. I can't say that I had that much interest in going to church at that time, but I sure did like riding in Mrs. Picket's buggy each Sunday, and playing with the other kids at church. Mrs. Picket was someone besides my Aunt Lula whom I learned to love and respect very much and have continued to hold in high regard.

It was about this time in my life that I started to gain more awareness of the world around me. There was more than town, school and church. I began to absorb a new vocabulary, words like stock market crash, President Herbert Hoover, Franklin Delano Roosevelt and the White House. There was also another change in my life. My family moved to a nicer house, which had four rooms and fewer cracks to let in the wind. It was going to be warmer there.

It didn't take long before "Depression" became a household word. Everybody talked about the Depression, but there was little change for me. I had been in a depression all of my life, possessing only the bare necessities: just enough food to keep from starving, just enough clothing to cover myself, and just enough of a roof over my head to keep from freezing. The Depression did not take anything from me because I had nothing to lose. Instead, it gave me things that were different from what I had been accustomed to having: government-issued cheese, raisins, oranges, beans, and other things that we needed or never had the opportunity to eat on a regular basis.

For some, living was better than ever before.

Life went on even during the Depression, just as it always had. One day followed another and we got up each morning and kept on living. My Uncle Fred told me that the first colt that his horse, Soralia, had was to be mine. No boy can forget his first pony. The colt was a very pretty reddish brown color. I named him Fox. Also about this time, my father gave me a German Shepherd puppy named Jack. This was the first gift I can remember receiving from my dad since he left me with Aunt Lula and Uncle Fred. Jack could hunt rabbits and he was quite playful. I loved my dog. For the next few years, my horse and dog provided most of my companionship.

There were neighbor kids I played and hunted with, but it was not until I met James Carthell Hayes that I learned about true friendship. We were the same age and in the same grade at school, but for some reason during this time we became like brothers, forming a friendship that lasted a lifetime, until his death seventy years later. I called him Carthell and he called me Gooch. One factor that likely figured in making us friends was that we both had slight speech problems: he stammered regularly and I had an inability to read aloud and pronounce a number of words. Other classmates and adults would make derogatory remarks about us. I would later puzzle over how Carthell could temporarily overcome his speech impediment to sing at his church.

We loved to pretend to be cowboys like we saw in the movies, riding horses and roping cattle. When the grown-ups went to town, we had a good time chasing cows to catch one to ride. One Saturday, I caught a bull, and rode him for a bit before he threw me and walked over me. My sides ached for a long while, and I was very sore. I couldn't tell anyone what had happened or I would have been in more trouble. I had to carry my share of the farm work as if nothing happened, in spite of the pain I was in.

When I was about ten years old, I began paying more attention to grown-up issues like politics. Voters around the country jumped on the Democratic band wagon to elect Franklin Roosevelt president over the Republican incumbent, Herbert Hoover. People spoke about how Roosevelt was going to change things. The year 1932 was one of great change in times and conditions. People heard abbreviations like WPA, NRA, CCC, NYA, and others I can't remember, but it was an exciting time for the underprivileged. These programs put people back to work and gave them hope for a future better than anything they ever had before. Black folks, who had always thought Republican because of Abraham Lincoln, became Democrats because of Franklin Roosevelt. I have to admit, though, that I was more excited about the two dogs the president and his wife owned than I was about becoming a Democrat. One of the animals was a German shepherd just like mine.

We all heard about the Civilian Conservation Corps camps, which provided young men with work at developing and conserving natural resources, but when those boys who had gone away to the camps came home in their yellow uniforms, whoo-wee! Everyone took notice — girls went crazy over those uniforms, and boys like Carthell and me, who were too young to attend CCC camps, just counted the months before we could go to camp and wear those uniforms so the girls would smile at us, too. We were waking up to the fact that girls were different from boys.

In this environment more poor people found the courage to leave the South and its sharecropping life. They went North alone, or as families if they could, to work in factories, to have better jobs and a better way of life. As new labor opportunities in steel mills, coal mines and other industries changed the North by attracting an invasion of poor people to already overcrowded cities like Detroit, Chicago and New York, the South also changed. The people who migrated loved to return home on vacation or for other occasions, bringing the North with them in cars, money and stories about how the move changed their lives. Relatives and friends from "up North" drove their new cars back home with pride. They wore the good clothes that good jobs allowed them to buy. They talked about the houses they lived in. Their cars had radios and convertible tops. Their down-home families were proud of what they were accomplishing in the North.

When members of my family described the house they had, they mentioned having a bathroom with an inside toilet. I could not imagine having an outhouse inside a house, nor that anyone would choose to have one. I thought the smell would be too terrible.

Sometimes well-to-do visitors encountered reminders that they were back in the South. One of Aunt Lula and Uncle Fred's relatives was driving around nearby Brownsville, Tennessee, with his radio on, showing off a bit, when Sheriff Billy Whitten stopped him and made him turn the radio off, "You're makin' too much noise, boy." He was fortunate Sheriff Whitten didn't arrest him. Whenever the manager of the Haywood County Prison Farm, Guy Harold, needed additional workers, he'd call the sheriff, who would then recruit "employees" by arresting blacks for any offense, including spitting on the floor. Sheriff Whitten was notorious enough for blues musician B.B. King to sing about him. A black man returning South had to remember that, down home, he was still a black man.

For those of us whose farm families couldn't uproot to travel North, working in the fields was a part of everyday life. I started working in the field about the same time I started school, and I had been working there for what seemed like forever. I knew the work had to be done routinely, but I began to think, "Is it something I want to be doing for the rest of my life?" I started to consider my future. As I worked, I did a lot of dreaming. Working with the hands leaves the mind free to wander and dream. My first dream was to own a farm with lots of land, lots of livestock and equipment. Later, watching planes fly over as I worked, my dreams took flight. I began to imagine myself up in the sky. I had never been in an airplane, but flying became my heart's desire. That dream would change my life and take me farther than I had the imagination and time to visualize. I had no concept of the height or distance within the grasp of air travel. Living east of Ripley, with my understanding of distance, it looked as if the sun went down in the evening between my house and town.

The house in which I grew up with my father's sister, Aunt Lula, and her husband, Fred Reed, when they sharecropped on the Walker farm in rural Lauderdale County, Tennessee.

Looking back at my early years, my dreams and the events that have motivated me to become the person I am today, I can point to one cold Christmas Eve as the spark that ignited everything I have done or dreamed of doing. Uncle Fred, Aunt Lula and I had driven our mule-drawn wagon to town to sell some produce to pay for some of our needs and a few Christmas presents. Hard times still prevailed and there wasn't much to sell from our farm except eggs, chickens and corn. We had gotten a late start on that cold day. Aunt Lula had put quilts in the wagon to keep us warm on the way home. We sold the produce, bought what we could and headed out of Ripley. Passing through the white section of town, we could see Christmas lights on in almost every home. We could also see all the gifts and food that those people had, which we didn't have. It was getting colder, and I probably should have covered up, but there was one big picture window that caught my attention. Looking in, I saw a family around a beautifully decorated Christmas tree, looking happy, warm and surrounded by presents.

I knew in my heart that was the kind of life I wanted for myself. Why was it that some people could have everything and other people so little or nothing? I could cover myself with the quilt that Aunt Lula had brought for the cold of that night, but there was no way to cover up the chill I felt inside. Would I always be poor, always needing something more than what I had? What determined who was on the inside and who was always on the outside looking in? When we returned home, I gathered wood to start a fire to warm the house, which had cracks too large to keep out the weather. I crawled into a cold bed and waited for Christmas. In the morning, we did not talk of what we lacked, knowing full well that there were many who had even less. We all smiled and were thankful.

Life on the farm rolled on in a predictable manner with a fixed agenda of work and play to fit the seasons. School was split into two sessions to accommodate growing and harvesting crops; there was no set 180-day education requirement. In the spring, we worked to prepare the fields for planting crops, and played around with horseback riding, Easter egg hunts and ball games. In the summer we mended fences and went to school, but still had time in that hot weather to swim and fish in the creek. Autumn was the busiest time of the year, when the major harvesting had to be done. It was also time to gather nuts and wild grapes for jelly and preserves. For men, it was time to start looking for the best hunting and trapping places for the winter ahead. I looked forward to the days of getting together with a number of the boys to go hunting with our dogs. The women stayed busy canning all that could be preserved and storing away that which could be dried and kept in sacks and jars. In the winter children returned to school, while men took care of the stock, butchering and curing meat to be stored in the smokehouse.

Rabbits in particular provided many people with food and income. I would set a couple of traps (wooden boxes with trap doors) every evening using turnips and lettuce as bait, check them the following morning before daylight and kill and dress the rabbits I'd caught. By the weekend, the three or four rabbits my family hadn't eaten remained frozen in our smokehouse, ready to be taken to town to be sold for their pelts and meat. Rabbits that were trapped rather than shot were more valuable because they'd have no bullet holes to fix. The rabbits would fetch about a quarter apiece at a time when a new pair of overalls cost a dollar. After President Roosevelt's New Deal reforms started doing some good one of my uncle's favorite comic strips, "Hambone," commented, "I don't know what happened, but I just saw a rabbit without anyone chasing it."

Preparing for the winter was a busy time and a supportive time. People helped one another in ways that seem to be forgotten today. What few skills we had were shared with one another, and what little else we had naturally also was shared. There was a lot of joy, story telling, laughter and singing. As I remember, people went about doing what they had to do. I chopped my wood and piled it and stacked it in the same spirit.

When I was about twelve, my family moved again, to a farm that was in a different school district. It was a small district school with only one room and just one teacher, Mr. John Wesley Halliburton, who had several children, including a son in my class. For one assignment we both had to draw pictures of a horse on the blackboard; I drew my picture and he drew his picture on top of mine, aiming to make it look like his horse was passing my horse. Mr. Halliburton thought we had deliberately drawn an indecent picture and he spanked us both.

As much as farming had taught me through the discipline of hard work that never seemed to end, there was still an emptiness within me that hungered for more than a life that would never look further than work and the seasons. I could never really put this into words, or talk to anyone about what was growing inside me like the seeds we planted each year. A restless hunger within me didn't allow me to be at peace with myself and things as they were. I wanted more.

During this period in my life I somehow ran across some old magazines. Among them were copies of Boy's Life, which glorified the activities and lifestyle of the Boy Scouts of America. To me, that magazine was the most exciting thing I had the privilege of reading. Most important to me was the fact that now I knew for sure there was another life beyond the one I'd known, and that it was within my reach. In Boy's Life, I saw things that related to my age. I saw boys sitting around campfires in uniforms with backpacks, and other pictures of camp life and Scout activities. As exciting as the photos were, it was the coupons in the magazine that opened up a new world to me by enabling me to send away for things I never knew I could have.

One coupon helped me acquire my first airplane. It offered a model airplane in exchange for selling Boy's Life subscriptions. I sold a few subscriptions, but it was with my Aunt Lula's help that enough subscriptions were sold for me to order the model plane. I mailed the coupon, and every day afterward I waited at our mailbox. It took only a few weeks, but it seemed like months before I held a tiny rubber-band-powered model airplane in my hands.

My travel had been limited, but everything I saw made me dream of the day when I could live a life in which just simple needs and desires, both material and physical, would be more attainable. I was thinking of a warm home, a well lit house in which to read and study, a school with a library, a basketball court and a chance to ride to school in a bus like the one that passed us black children by and picked up the white kids.

It was during this time that Aunt Lula tried to teach me that spiritual values were as much needed as material possessions. Being a mother to me for most of my life, Aunt Lula knew me probably better than I knew myself. What I was feeling about life was not a new experience for her. She knew my desires for material things could be my enemy as well as my friend. My spiritual mother told me to be thankful for what I had, for where I was, and who I was. In her way, she was trying to tell me that a better life is not something one pines for like a child, but something that must be accomplished by working for it and, by God's grace, accepting that which cannot be changed.

She taught me the Three D's: Dedication, Determination, De Lord.

These Three D's had helped Aunt Lula and Uncle Fred make peace with the sharecropping life, which was not stable. We moved yet again during this period, back to the school district that I previously attended, with the three-room school building and three teachers. I was glad to return to the school for my eighth-grade year so I could graduate with friends. This time, conditions were better under Principal Lillie V. Jones, a young, beautiful, recently graduated teacher from Memphis. She was able to arrange a bus trip to the Memphis City Zoo for her students, on a Thursday, the only day Negroes were allowed to visit the zoo. It was the first field trip we ever experienced. Principal Jones also bought us our first basketball, from proceeds raised by having the students sell candy.

This turned out to be the last year I spent with Aunt Lula and Uncle Fred, and it was a pleasant one. I had come to know Uncle Fred well and think of him as a father. I also began to think of myself as being almost a man, and started wanting more things of my own. Both Aunt Lula and Uncle Fred encouraged me about what they thought I should do. My aunt said I should plant a garden to sell produce to make some money of my own. I followed her advice. I was quite happy and proud of myself for what my industry accomplished, but there was one problem: I had no way to transport my produce to market. I have heard it said so many times that when you can't see your way through a problem you can make a way or find a way. At this point in my life, the way found me. Benny Lee, a member of my family's church congregation, whose wife, I later found out, was a cousin to my mother, worked as a regular produce street vendor in nearby Ripley. He often drove by our house en route to town and eventually saw what I was trying to do, and he allowed me to sell my wares out of the back of his truck while he stood beside me selling his. I received my first sales training from Mr. Benny, and I will forever be thankful to him for his aid and guidance. From this experience I started my first bank account.

Benny Lee, shown here at age 95 in 2006, taught me how to sell my farm produce, which allowed me to open my first bank account in the 1930s.

The same summer, the year of my sixteenth birthday and my eighth-grade graduation, provided another turning point in my life. The Christian training that I had received from my aunt, Mrs. Picket and others began to take a real place in my life. I had previously listened with deaf ears while people spoke of their religion and faith. As I began to realize I needed more things of my own, I also began to realize that I needed my own relationship with God. I invited Him into my life at the Elam Baptist Church, in Durhamville, a tiny community outside Ripley. In the Baptist Church one has to make a public confession of faith, and during a Sunday service, I gave my life to Christ. I do not claim that confession of faith or a relationship with God has made me lead a perfect life, but I know I have never forgotten there is a power much greater than man.

It was also in the Elam Baptist Church that I received an epiphany that was more motivational than spiritual. On April 28, 1939, I graduated from eighth grade second in my class of six students. My ranking in the class of four girls and two boys (my best friend Jim Carthell Hayes and I) had little value to anyone except myself. At that time, graduating from eighth grade was about all the education that was expected for a boy from a poor family. By finishing school, I had honored my aunt and uncle, who had given me a home and raised me as their own child. Aunt Lula and Uncle Fred were very proud of what they had helped me achieve. By graduating, I had done what they never had the chance to do; like most of the people we knew – sharecroppers and farm hands – just making a living was a constant lifetime struggle day in and day out, and school was not necessary.

The people who attended our graduation also had very little "schooling," as they called it, but they thought well of those who did. The six of us graduates reveled in that respect; graduation was our night of honor. Most of us had been in school together since first grade and had seen a number of other young people attend class only to drop out later. Not everyone who had started school with us held education in high regard. They didn't see how "book learning" was going to change their lives. I can't say I was always certain that a lot of it wasn't a waste of time – with racist books such as *Tales of Uncle Remus, Uncle Tom's Cabin* and *The Little Black Tar Baby* – but I'm glad I stayed in school.

The church was crowded with family and congregation members who wished all the class well. The community took pride in seeing young people making progress. They were thankful that times were changing and that they had lived to see the younger generation benefit. The graduation speaker was Rev. R. G. Murray. We all knew Rev. Murray, and he knew each one of our families and us. He spoke to us as if we were his children. His subject that night was "Aim High." I don't remember all that he said, but I felt that he was talking about something he had regretted about his life. He was not asking us, but telling us, that our future was our choice – "Aim High." I forever regarded that motivational boost as one of the key events in my development. I have never ceased to measure my life by the level of my aim.

—Reflections—

Ready to start high school.

Chapter 4
A Real Education

My first year out of grade school I lived about eight miles from the nearest high school, which was in Ripley. My motivation to continue my education was strong enough that I tried to commute back and forth to class.

The high school was nothing to brag about, but it provided something, even if we had to learn Shakespeare, which I felt was a waste of time. The only subject I liked was what I could do best, and that was math. English and reading didn't appeal to me, maybe because the school's library was so lackluster. It took up a couple of shelves in a corner of the principal's office. I had never seen a "library" before, and I sure wasn't impressed. We had a set of encyclopedias that was missing a volume or two; it was, like most of the books, formerly used and abused at a white school and then handed down to us. In retrospect, I can see how obvious it was that the educational material presented to us was oriented to white students because that was the standard the U.S. Department of Education had established.

On the bright side, I made a number of new friends in school. I found out that many of them – such as Alan Searcy, Anna Fay Macklin, Samuel Lee and Josephine Perkins – were much better prepared than I for getting an education, mainly because they came from families that included teachers or successful business people.

Naturally, at that time we had a problem with busing, the problem being that they didn't pick up black kids. I had to leave home early enough every morning to try to hitchhike a ride to make it to school eight miles away. I often got to school late, past the first class. At one point I tried to fix the situation by assembling a bicycle from parts I'd found. The tires were well worn, and I couldn't afford new ones, so when they went flat I resumed walking. It was an extension of my difficulties in seeking a quality education – after enduring grades one through eight, I was now wanting and trying to get to high school everyday but still missing class.

Come winter I started staying with another of my father's sisters, Aunt Mary, who lived in Ripley and only about a mile from school. When the weather grew harsh, I often stopped at Mary's rather than brave the freezing eight-mile trek to Aunt Lula's. My stays with Mary became so frequent I decided to just live with her during the winter school session, returning to Aunt Lula's home in March or April. Next to my father, Mary was the youngest of Sam Thomas

Gooch's children. She was widowed at the time I lodged with her, but she had a grown son living at home and a daughter who'd married and moved to Chicago. Mary's son, James, served as a sort of mentor to me in real-life matters because he was several years older. I admired the way he was able to draw women to himself. He did not attend school past the eighth grade and worked a series of menial jobs. Though James did not encourage my education or help me study, his then-job as a gas station attendant showed me that I needed school to allow me to achieve my goals in life.

Directly across the street from Aunt Mary lived one of my teachers, from whom I would often catch a ride. Franklin Rhodes and his wife Julia, who taught at the elementary school, became good friends to me. I still visit Franklin when I get back to Tennessee every year or so. At this writing, he is 95 and still sharp, even driving himself around. He has said that he considered me a good student, but I still struggled with balancing education with commuting and working. I was determined I wanted to do something better. Opportunity showed itself during the summer following my first year of high school, in the person of an acquaintance of my Aunt Lula's.

Franklin Rhodes, science teacher at Lauderdale County Training School (the county's black high school), often gave me rides to school.

In addition to working on the farm, Aunt Lula earned spare money as a practical nurse helping sick or recuperating people in the area. Through this work, she became familiar with a young white lady named Amelia Rice, who was married to a local farm equipment dealer. She would drive out to our farm to visit once in a while; I think it was as much to raid the vegetable garden as it was to visit - she always ended up with a collection of whatever was in season. At some point Aunt Lula mentioned to her that I was having a difficult time getting to school. Mrs. Rice, who had been a teacher before she married and was living about six miles from the high school, understood the situation and said she'd like to have somebody to help out around her house and offered to ask her husband's permission to give me the job. Mr. Rice agreed.

The Rice family resided in Henning, the town that later became known as the setting of Alex Haley's book *Roots*. With the Rices I worked in exchange for food and shelter, and showed up in class on time because a school bus was finally making the rounds. A Hennings minister/grade school principal by the name of L. "Bear" Nelson, a man respected by the people in the county, had raised funds to build a bus. He had a unique way of collecting the money: if folks didn't have cash he'd accept chickens, corn and the like and then sell those things. The Rev. Nelson thought the young people in outlying areas who wanted an education shouldn't be hindered by not being able to get to school. He paid some carpenter friends to fix up a makeshift bus by building a wooden cab that could sit on the back end of a truck he'd purchased with the donations. The bus, steered by one of the high school seniors, would drive around the rural area of Ripley to pick up black kids. By the time I started riding it an addition had already been put on the original bus, and soon after, another bus was put into operation.

The homemade bus that carried the black high school students of rural Lauderdale County to class in the 1930s and beyond.

Ready to begin my second year of high school, I was totally separated from all my family members. I arrived at my new home with the few belongings I had carried in a knapsack, and found that Mr. Rice had cleaned out the roughly eight-by-twenty foot windowless tool shed adjoining his garage for me. In it were a fabric folding cot and a couple of apple crates to put things on, a light bulb hanging from the ceiling and a small electric heater. There was one door. The building still stands, and it looks as ramshackle as it did when I lived in it. I worked in the Rice home and in the yard, cleaning and cooking and if they ran short of help, I'd assist with the grainery and farm equipment.

Staying with the Rices did help; I could wash dishes and run down the street to where the bus stopped. Sometimes I'd be late catching the bus and Mrs. Rice would drive me in the family's 1937 Ford to the next stop. If we missed the bus completely, we would wave it down and the driver would let me get on. If that didn't work, Mrs. Rice would take me the five miles to school. She eventually drove me to Ripley to get a driver's license so I could occasionally take myself to school. The state highway patrolman who issued licenses hesitated. Trying to use her family's influence, Mrs. Rice told the officer, "He can drive; give him a license." The patrolman demanded that they at least have me drive around the block to see how I'd do.

I never heard about it until later, but evidently some people criticized my being driven by Mrs. Rice as well as my driving her car. Whether she knew about the criticism or not, by the end of the year we both decided keeping up our schedule was quite a struggle. Mrs. Rice negotiated another job for me, with a family who lived in Ripley and owned a combination grocery and appliance store and a large farm machinery sales business, as well as quite a bit of land. Another change for me was that I would live in a room rented from an elderly widow in the black part of town rather than on the family's property.

The Eugene Anthony family was in the upper social echelon of the county, and that put me in a prime position to make some extra money. At 17, my situation was finally starting to brighten. I was out living by myself, with nobody controlling me. With the Rices I'd get done with my chores and go to bed directly because they could observe my routine, but now I was living across town from my employers. The Anthonys had full-time house help, too, which allowed me free time for personal business. Occasionally, I'd get off work from the Anthonys' in the evening and walk into the hard part of town to make some extra money – shooting craps, playing pool, gambling. You had to learn not to compete with the mature hustlers who didn't do much of anything else – you had to sort of operate on their fringes. My specialty was craps, and I targeted young guys who didn't know enough not to waste their money, guys who often had dropped out of school by the eighth grade.

The country folks would converge on Ripley on Saturday night. Hired hands, sharecroppers, anyone, no matter how poor, made sure to have a little money for the weekend, and the locals would stand by and look for ways to rip them off. In the area referred to as the Hole, which was home to a number of black businesses, there was the popular Betty Rogers Hotel & Restaurant, which had three sections: a pool hall and a restaurant on ground level, and a quickie hotel on the upper level. Folks would go in there to play pool, drink beer, get a plate lunch for a quarter, and, if they could, negotiate a commitment and head upstairs.

Another occasional activity for me was chasing women, particularly older women. I'd hit the street and might not get in before midnight, or might just not leave some lady's place until going to the Anthonys' house the next morning. One night, a school friend and I hooked up with a couple of women in their twenties and went over to their house. We stayed fairly late, when somebody came knocking at the door. We waited for the knocking to stop before my friend looked out the window, and saw his dad. His pop was probably coming to make out with one of those ladies! We were careful whom we told that story around.

Admittedly, I occasionally hung out in rough territory, which I guess was one of the reasons I ended up buying a Smith and Wesson revolver. I'm glad nobody ever made me use it.

There wasn't any real encouragement to go home and study. Mr. Anthony came home drunk sometimes and would go on a binge in his bedroom. Occasionally, he'd call me to his room, give me money and send me to buy whiskey. Now, there was an opportunity! Lauderdale County was dry, with the exception of beer, but the counties on both sides permitted the sale of alcohol. I would drive Mr. Anthony's car, a fairly new 1940 Buick, south across the Hatchie River into Tipton County and purchase liquor for him. The Lauderdale County sheriff and deputies would often lie in wait on their side of the river waiting for cars with black drivers to come over looking like they might be carrying whiskey, but they never stopped me. I was working for one of the men who called the shots in town. It wasn't long before I started driving Mr. Anthony's car to Tipton County to haul whiskey back for local bootleggers, too.

After I became accustomed to smuggling booze, I moved into dealing it. I'd get four gallons of wine for about five dollars, and split it into half-pint bottles. I recruited other reckless youngsters to sell these half-pints for me in the high school gym during basketball games and other functions for 25 cents a bottle. My salesmen pocketed a nickel a bottle and I'd get 20 cents. The young customers would pay for a couple half-pints and go out in the crowd and show off. They'd take a few sips and stride around trying to act bad, breathing in folks' faces and telling them they'd been out drinking.

A diminutive friend of mine, Abraham Currie, would wander around under the gym bleachers selling these half-pint bottles. He would put four or five in his belt, put his coat on and get down to business. One night while our school was playing an opponent from an adjoining county, somebody shot a basket that tied up the net. The principal, who was tall, stood under the hoop but couldn't reach the net, and then Abraham entered the gym with the bottles hidden in his belt. "Hey, boy! Come here," Principal S.H. Johnson called. He boosted Abraham up, and I nearly busted a gut laughing, waiting for the bottles to fall out of Abraham's pants.

"Reach up there, boy!"

Abraham wouldn't extend his arms to reach the net because he feared dropping his bottles; he kept his elbows down, as if his armpits smelled.

"I can't reach it!"

"Reach up there, boy!"

Abraham was one of those guys who never pursued higher education. He became an over-the-road truck driver, and the last time I saw him he was drunkenly busy embarrassing our female high school classmates at a reunion. I don't know if I pulled him down when he should have been going up, but we always laughed about the fun times we had in our younger days.

A few incidents in my life have really changed me, but the one that really made me do an about-face was shooting a gun at a high school social. The spring of my junior year, the students decided to hold a junior-senior prom. A formal get-together was organized at the school, and afterward we gathered for cookies and ice cream at the home of a female classmate whose mother was an elementary teacher. The house was near our high school and also, unfortunately, near the residence of our principal.

My contribution to the party was some wine. My partner in crime, Abraham Currie, and I brought enough for everybody at the party to smell as if they'd had a drink. People were mingling in the house and on the porch and feeling swell when Abraham, who'd likely had more than a few sips and wanted to impress the porch crowd, pulled out a gun and said, "I feel like I ought to just shoot my pistol."

"You hear that – Abraham's gonna shoot his pistol!" everyone gasped.

"Yes, I've got a pistol and I'm going to shoot it," Abraham said slowly and deliberately.

Now, I'd had a gun for some time – for protection – but had never had reason to use it, and no one knew I had it. Seeing a chance to upstage my pal with my .32 caliber revolver, I said, "Well, Abraham, I got one too."

"What? Gooch got a gun? Did you know Gooch had a gun?" our friends whispered.

"Abraham, if you shoot your pistol, I'm going to shoot my pistol," I said.

Abraham pulled his weapon's trigger, and it went "snip." Then I pulled my weapon's trigger … and it went "boom"!

"Put that piece of junk back in your pocket; it won't even shoot," I gloated.

Around this time the principal's wife was walking down the street with a friend, returning home from a movie. She overheard some of the commotion, including someone saying, "That was Gooch's pistol that was shootin'!" Monday morning, when I got to school, I was not popular. Word had gotten to the principal. Not long after my arrival, in fact, the teacher told me Professor Johnson wanted to see me in his office. Luckily, I had left my pistol at home.

Lauderdale County Training School principal S.H. Johnson changed the course of my life with a short discussion after I shot a gun at a school social.

S.H. Johnson was only about 45, but he was ancient to us. He was very well thought of in the area, physically strong, well educated and smart. He demanded respect. The school kids all called him "Snake" because he was thin and tall. I felt small walking into that office to face him, but I had to go. "Sir, I did something bad."

'Gooch, I'm sorry to hear that," he said.

I apologized and explained my circumstances: I was living by myself in a rough part of town, trying to survive, and doing things that I was not necessarily proud of to make some money or to get some entertainment.

"You know you've got a lot of potential in you, and the fact that you're on your own is admirable, but you've got to get yourself together," Professor Johnson said. "Your parents think an awful lot of you. It's not too late for you to get back on track."

At that time we had occasional morning assemblies at the school to discuss matters that might affect us all, such as when Pearl Harbor was bombed, and Professor Johnson told us some students might get called up for service and not come back. Following my visit to his office over that gunshot, everyone gathered in the upstairs auditorium to hear him address the hot topic. "I'm sure you've all heard about an incident that occurred over the weekend," Principal Johnson said. "I have visited with the student responsible and we have gotten some things straightened out. I'm not proud of what the person did, and neither is the person proud of what he did, but we are going to proceed from here as if nothing happened. It has been taken care of. That's all there is to say."

He never mentioned my name. He never looked at me. I've never forgotten the way he handled that, and I admired him for sparing me further embarrassment. Looking back many years later, I have to think that had Professor Johnson expelled me, I would not have followed the path in life I did. Perhaps I'd have kept working for the Anthonys, started drinking whiskey, remained a farmhand and turned out like my father.

Chapter 5
Determination

During the summer of 1942, the break after my junior year of high school, and following my encounter with the principal over that gunshot, I heard that the military was looking for workers to build bases, and would pay more than I was making from the Anthonys. Jim Carthell Hayes and I applied and were hired to do construction work on the first base built in western Tennessee, Millington Naval Air Station, thirty miles south of Ripley and about 20 miles north of Memphis on 51 Highway. We rented a room from a family in Millington, and occasionally carpooled to Ripley with other people we knew.

The nation's involvement in World War II necessitated building bases to train troops to fight. Starting in 1941 and 1942 military installations popped up around the country like popcorn. This wartime construction boom provided work for so many people and companies that it effectively ended the Great Depression.

When fall came and our senior year of high school started, Carthell and I left Millington to work at Dyersburg Army Air Base, which was being built at Halls, Tennessee, about ten miles north of Ripley and five miles south of Dyersburg. Fully aware that we would be well served to attempt to graduate high school before possibly being drafted into the military, Carthell and I transferred so that we could attend class during the day and work at night. I decided to purchase a vehicle for the commute, a '32 Chevy sedan that had been sitting in someone's yard needing repairs. Carthell, who always hung out around garages and later became a very good mechanic, promptly decided to overhaul the car. He tightened the rods on the crankshaft so much that they prevented us from starting the engine, though we didn't realize that was our problem. We bought a new battery, but that didn't work. As a last resort, Jim loosened the rods and we discovered that if we pushed the car, it started and would keep running. Every time we'd stop, though, the Chevy would need oil – bulk quantities of it. Soon, a five-gallon oil can became our third passenger. One night we started home from the base, Carthell at the wheel. I thought I'd take a nap, and then – wing, bing, bang! I woke up and saw sparks flying.

"We hit something?" I asked

"No, I'd have seen it." Carthell replied

We got out to look at the engine – a rod had come all the way out of the crank case and was sticking out the side. Carthell, with his speech problem, stuttered and pointed, "I-I-I don't remember th-th-that being th-th-there." Our ride was out of commission. The knife in our wound twisted a bit when we thought about our brand new tires. Meat, gas, rubber, metal, paper and other items were rationed during the war, and anyone with access to such supplies enjoyed a status boost. Carthell and I acquired our tires via working on the military base, so we grew discouraged at the thought of having nice tires but no car on which to show them off.

Working at night and attending school in the daytime started eating on me after a few months. I didn't know how I was going to continue the schedule and was feeling overburdened when I had an idea that would be my salvation. There were two powerful black newspapers at that time, the Chicago Defender and the Pittsburgh Courier, which were distributed around the country, and I'd pick up copies now and then and see pictures of guys in flight suits standing next to their beautiful airplanes. It was really exciting for me because I always wanted to fly, and here were men just like me flying. The papers said the Tuskegee Institute was where these people were.

Due to segregation in the armed services the all-black Tuskegee Institute's Moton Airfield, a few miles outside Tuskegee, Alabama, was the only place in the nation at that time where African-Americans could train to become military pilots. Prior to World War II blacks were not even allowed to be military pilots, though a small number of them had taken up aviation as a hobby since the 1920s, and a portion of them trained in the civilian flight training program at the Tuskegee Institute and in a few other primarily black programs at universities and airports around the country.

In the military blacks were relegated to posts as servants or janitors. That started to change when First Lady Eleanor Roosevelt visited the Tuskegee Institute around 1940 and met C. Alfred "Chief" Anderson, the head of the flight training program there and the man considered the father of black aviation. Against the Secret Service's suggestions for her safety, the First Lady allowed Chief Anderson to fly her around the institute's grounds to demonstrate that blacks were as capable as whites to operate aircraft. At the First Lady's insistence, President Roosevelt mandated that blacks be allowed to fly in the military. The military opposed the move, then compromised, agreeing to allow blacks to train at only one location, a base called Tuskegee Army Air Base, to be built near the Tuskegee Institute. Until the base was completed, cadets trained with the institute's civilian program. Qualifications were very stringent for black cadets at Tuskegee. Those rejected from the Tuskegee flight training program were sent to the infantry to fight or to another air base to wash planes and serve food to white servicemen. The roughly 900 men who graduated from the training program during its four-year existence became known as the Tuskegee Airmen, one of the most elite groups in America's black society.

My car was busted and I had no way to travel back and forth to work and school, so I decided to go to the Tuskegee Institute and help fly airplanes. I had no knowledge of how to go about becoming a pilot; I didn't have anyone available to teach me and a lot of people would look at me like I was crazy if I mentioned my interest. Because I knew no blacks who cared about aviation, I thought Tuskegee would have trouble finding recruits. I decided to travel there riding freight trains and hitchhiking, first riding a box car to Memphis, then thumbing down the highway.

When I arrived in Tuskegee, I asked around as to where I could sign up to fly planes, and was pointed toward Tuskegee Institute a couple of miles or so out of town on an old plantation. At the school someone gave me a ride several miles farther to Moton Airfield, where the institute's flight program was located. Here civilian instructors would provide military cadets their initial lessons, prior to moving on to additional training at Tuskegee Army Airfield.

I told them I came from Tennessee and wanted to join the army flight training program.

"You can't get in this way," a man told me. "You have to take some tests and get on the list."

"A list? There's a war going on and I want to fly, and there are bases all over. What's the problem?" I asked.

"You see, there's only one base in the United States where we have colored people starting military flight training. All those bases around that you're talking about, you can't get in there. There'd be no problem if you could train at any air base. We probably got a thousand people who want to be here just like you. You go back home, and tell them you want to be in the Army Air Corps and take the test."

I stayed on the campus a couple of days, looked around and met people. The newspaper pictures I'd seen had not done justice to the actual experience of seeing real people and real airplanes. Somehow I crossed paths with C. Alfred Anderson, known as "Chief" because he was the chief flight instructor at the institute.

"You ever been up in a plane, boy," Chief asked me.

"No, sir," I said, without a clue as to how significant a figure he was.

"Well, we're going to take you for a ride."

That first taste of flying, in an open-cockpit biplane, scared me, amazed me and thrilled me. To have been piloted by one of the most significant black aviators around made the experience perfect, but I would not appreciate that until years later. In the future, in fact, I would eventually become good friends with Chief and a number of other Tuskegee Airmen.

Ultimately, seeing people of color flying airplanes encouraged me and left me determined that even though I would be going home, I was going to pursue every possible means of becoming a pilot. Of course, I thought it would take only a few weeks and a visit to a recruiting office to take a test. I headed back to Ripley and back to school. In all, I had been away for about a week. I told the principal where I had gone and everything was all right. Not long after, though, I decided to go to Memphis, where I could take those tests and get my name on the pilot entry list. As I approached the federal office building, I could see the motivational signs: "We need you," "Join up." I walked in motivated, a country boy in the big city ready to serve my country. In the office, a large white man with shiny brass on his uniform and stripes on his arm addressed me, "What you want, boy?"

"I want to join the Army Air Corps to fly airplanes."

That guy started laughing, and the more he laughed, the smaller I felt until I didn't think I'd be able to see over the counter that separated us.

"You know what?" he called into a back room where a lieutenant was working. "We got a boy here who wants to fly airplanes!"

The lieutenant, who knew from what the fat man yelled that I was black, said, "You know they got a place now they're letting them learn to fly airplanes? They don't know what they're going to do with them, but they're going to let some of them fly.

"We have to let them go through; we let that other boy take a test. Orders from the government that we need to do something."

"I didn't know that," the fat man said.

They told me to come back on an appointed day and time to take the test, but by the time I saved money for the bus trip and returned to Memphis, the whole situation disgusted me. Remembering that the folks at Tuskegee said I could take the test after entering the military, I volunteered for service. It wasn't until I was sent through enlisted procedure that I realized they never gave me credit for volunteering; I had been registered as a draftee. I found this out when someone looked at my serial number, which designated the difference, and told me. What likely happened was that whoever filed my paperwork moved my name up on the draft list rather than reflecting that I had volunteered.

Additionally, I missed the last months of my senior year of high school and did not graduate. Luckily, I had a good friend in science teacher Franklin Rhodes – he persuaded the school officials to ignore my final-semester absence due to my joining the military. I was awarded my diploma on one of my trips home on leave. It was a gesture that affected me much the same way I was affected by S.H. Johnson's treatment of my gun-shooting incident. Had I not received that diploma through Mr. Rhodes' intervention, I would not have returned to high school or gone to college.

Teacher Franklin Rhodes convinced school officials to award a high school diploma to me even though I missed my final semester by joining the military in 1943.

—*Reflections*—

In a Memphis photo studio shortly after my 1943 military induction.

Chapter 6
In the Army Now

For more than a year following my military induction on February 9, 1943, I was stationed several miles outside Greenville, Texas, at Majors Army Airfield, with the all-new, all-colored 332nd Aviation Service Squadron. This unit was among the first stationed at Greenville, and service was the job of this group – food and table service for the cadets and officers (all of whom were white), cleaning service for the general officers' quarters, and washing of and general service for airplanes. The duties matched the area's expectations of blacks.

For a long time Greenville (1943 population about 6,000), county seat of Hunt County in northeast Texas, displayed a big banner from its bus terminal to the Texaco station across the highway that served as the main drag: "Welcome to Greenville – The blackest land – The whitest people."

That was right on the money.

Postcard of Greenville, Texas, in the 1940s, home of Majors Army Airfield. Note that the banner reads: "The Blackest Land, The Whitest People."

The extremely fertile soil was as dark as dirt comes, and many locals matched the stereotype of Southern bigotry that was prevalent in that era. Greenville's big boast now is that its post office was the place where Audie Murphy, the most decorated soldier of World War II and future movie star, enlisted in the Army. Decades ago, though, Greenville was a town proud of such moments as the 1908 public burning of eighteen-year-old African-American Ted Smith, who had been accused of assaulting a young white woman; photo postcards of the town-square event, complete with onlookers in the background, circulated for years.

Although it was rumored that the base was set up near Greenville to accommodate commanding officer Col. Herbert Newstrom, a native of the area, the site was actually chosen in 1938 by the town's Rotary Club as a good spot for a municipal airport. In early 1942, after the United States joined the war and while airport construction was already under way, Greenville's Chamber of Commerce pushed for the government to lease the complex as an Army Air Corps training school, probably to offset the airfield's $6 million construction cost. The Chamber's efforts were probably helped by the powerful congressman Sam Rayburn, an alumnus of the nearby East Texas State University.

As a military installation, Majors Field was one of 149 areas approved by the Civil Aeronautics Authority as an army flight-training center, and one of a number of bases that housed colored non-flying "aviation squadrons." The term "aviation squadron" was designated by the Air Corps' head, Gen. "Hap" Arnold, as a way of integrating the Air Corps (as per Congressional decree) without letting blacks fly, except at Tuskegee. We could do maintenance work on aircraft, but we couldn't operate them – even when our names were put on the list to start cadet training.

Right away when I hit Greenville I made it clear my goal was to go into flight training and, just like a number of other guys, I took the test to qualify. By fall 1944, in addition to being in charge of physical training, I had been working on the flight line servicing airplanes, so I was learning quite a bit about the aircraft. Neither a high test score nor experience, though, meant I was going to be a pilot. A white soldier on line service, who was also on the list for cadet training, later supplied me with information confirming this. He was called to report and saw my name and someone else's on the list above him. He asked the person in charge whether the other guy and I were going to start training, and that person said, "No, not now, not ever. The colonel said they ain't never going to because the colored got no business flying."

The information upset me so much I asked for a transfer, hoping to go to another air base. In only a few weeks orders came sending me into the infantry, completely out of the Army Air Corps.

In Greenville, we used to have a problem getting off base for recreation, for

Some of the members of the service squadron based at Majors Army Airfield in Greenville, Texas, during World War II. I'm on the far right. We were not allowed to learn to pilot any aircraft, only wash and service them.

a reason I heard from the white service guys, who most likely knew what was going on. Looking back, the explanation makes sense. As the airfield's commanding officer, Col. Newstrom carried a certain amount of influence in the town. Often when the community held social functions, someone would ask the colonel not to allow his soldiers off the base, and we'd be told no passes were available. On occasion, though, the base would hold a dance and send buses to outlying towns to pick up women for us to dance with.

Although we couldn't always get into Greenville, we could sign up to fly with instructor pilots who were going to other cities for a day or more. Destinations could be close, like Houston, or further away, like Memphis. Normal circumstances for such trips involved an instructor pilot having someplace he'd like to go. He could have some cadets tag along if they needed cross-country formation training. Our planes were 450-horsepower BT13 training aircraft, with space for a student in the front seat and an instructor in back. In one particular case, an instructor from Memphis and another instructor wanted to fly there for a weekend to chase women. To make the trip official, they arranged for some of their cadets to fly a formation day flight there, and a formation night flight back. With one formation for each instructor, each with two student pilots, that meant a total of six planes. Though cadets could not carry passengers, instructors could, so that left room for service personnel like me and George Harris, a fellow Tennesseean I'd met, to ride along.

We arrived in Memphis without a problem during the daytime on a Friday. Though I stayed with my sister Christine, who had lived there for some time, George and I spent most of our trip hanging out in a section of town known as Orange Mound, where the upwardly mobile blacks were settled including some of George's relatives. The neighborhood had its own movie theater, drug store and many pretty girls.

By the time we were ready to leave on Sunday, a hailstorm had knocked holes in our planes' fabric control surfaces (the ailerons, elevators, rudder; the rest of the plane was metal). We spotted the holes when we were ready to return to Greenville. Due to the holes, the airport maintenance crew wouldn't authorize flight, and because we wanted to spend more time in town anyway, the head instructor pilot called Greenville to say we were going to be detained due to the hail damage to the planes. We stayed a couple of days longer, until the instructor pilots were ready to leave, and then went to the airfield, patched the planes ourselves and took off.

Another jaunt resulted in me avoiding Dallas for quite a while.

My friend Fred Goodman and I signed up for an overnight trip, leaving on a Friday evening and returning the next morning. We hooked up with a couple of gals and had fun boozing up on Central Track, at that time one of the main nightlife areas for blacks in Dallas. Eventually, we split – Fred with his lady, I with mine. My companion took me to her room, and then told me how much she would cost for the rest of the evening. Already being there and ready, I was not going to refuse; confronted with an offer of not more than five dollars, I paid.

I napped off quickly afterward, having drunk a fair amount of booze. A while later I noticed this girl getting out of bed, but I didn't give any indication I was waking. She came over to the dresser beside me, took my billfold and grabbed my money, then walked to the coal-burning fireplace near the foot of the bed, removed a loose brick and put my money under it then quietly came back to bed.

Not long after she returned to bed she started snoring. I slipped out from the covers and put on my clothes. Locating and lifting the loose brick, I found my money and quite a bit more, about fifty dollars. I took it all. By that time it was close to 4 a.m.; the pilots, Fred and I were to leave in about three hours. I caught a cab to the base and waited at the flight ready room.

Fred ran into the ready room near departure time, yelling, "I am never coming to Dallas again with you, Gooch! That woman you were with found me and followed me to the gate! She is out there waiting to get you if you showed up, and she wanted to hold me there until you showed!"

Evidently, Fred didn't know I had returned to the base early and, looking for me, he waited until the last minute to report for the trip home. Whenever I traveled after that experience, I made sure to steer clear of Dallas, and managed to for about twenty-five years.

—Reflections—

Jesse Joyner (bottom left) introduced me (top left) to my second love, Fay Hill, in 1943 in Greenville, Texas.

Chapter 7
Fay Hill

My first love had been a quiet, smart girl who attended my high school, James Ella Turner. Whether due to my wild life at the time or her reserved nature, our relationship was never a deep one over the three years we were close. She didn't seem to care as deeply for me as I for her, and after I joined the military and returned on occasion, I noticed she'd taken up company with another of our classmates, with whom she would attend college and later marry. Though they made a fine couple (both teachers), I felt heartbroken at the time, but the situation made way for me to meet my second love, one of the few rays of light in my time in Texas, Fay Hill.

Fay graduated high school about the time I arrived at Majors Army Airfield, and was a regular teeny-bopper. I started dating her and got carried away. It was her mother, though, whom I really grew to love. Miss Lillian was loving, kind and motherly, which meant a lot to me because I was away from home and missed my family. She was a single mother of three; her son, the oldest of the children, was already in the army, stationed at Fort Riley, Kansas.

I met Fay through Jesse Joyner, a service friend who was dating her older sister. We all would run around together, play cards and dance. Once in awhile, Jesse and I would pool our liquor ration stamps and visit a store in Greenville that carried some of the good whiskey that was more readily available to military personnel than to regular folks. We'd buy all we could with our ration stamps because the stores often let us purchase the good stuff only if we bought some of their second-rate stuff too. Only after we ran out of our good whiskey did we consume the rotgut whiskey, gin and rum.

One of three times in my life that I've gotten outright skunked involved a fifth of rotgut rum consumed on a Greenville excursion. Having finished off some fine-grade bourbon, Jesse and I were working on the rest of our liquor supply in the Hills' living room while Miss Lillian was at work at the local hospital. Now, the Hill girls never drank and had no interest in drinking, but they tolerated Jesse and me. He and Fay's sister decided to go out somewhere dancing or partying and left Fay and me at the house along with the last part of a bottle of rotgut rum. I sipped on it awhile, and then my head started to go around; I don't know if I finished the bottle, but I got sick. I threw up until there was nothing left and threw up some more. Soon, red stuff was coming out of me. Fay called her mother, who said to give me tomato juice. With the tomato juice being coughed back up with blood, Fay grew extremely worried, and when I finally became unconscious she panicked.

Miss Lillian came home immediately and took charge, unbeknownst to me.

I awoke early in the morning on Sunday in Fay's room, in her bed, wondering what happened. I couldn't piece together events since the last thing I remembered. This won't be good when her mama gets home from work, I thought. The longer I lay there, the more I considered escaping: The sun was shining and Lillian was supposed to be home, so I was in the wrong place. As nice a lady as she was, I didn't want to try to explain that situation. I could get out the window – no, I decided, I'll just take another nap. Finally, a couple of hours later, Fay came in and woke me, "Mama is making breakfast and wants you there."

"I ain't going in there, baby!"

"She ain't mad – she and I put you here. It was her idea."

Well, I figured I'd face the music. Fay's mama was as nice as pie. After breakfast she entered the kitchen well dressed, saying, "I'm going to church. I'll see you all later!" Thereafter, I would always keep myself straight with Miss Lillian. She handled that situation with class.

I was really hooked on Fay for about a year and a half. When I was transferred to the infantry, I shipped out and lost contact. Later, I ran into somebody who said, "A year after you left, she married Edgar Evans. She figured you were going overseas and she'd never see you again." Edgar Evans was one of my army cohorts at Majors.

In the early 1970s, I was attending a convention in Atlanta, Georgia. Because I knew Fay's husband was from there, I decided to try to find him and Fay. Edgar had passed away several years prior, but I found Fay and we had a nice visit. She told me she worked as a beautician for a long time, and Edgar had joined the postal service when he left the military. When my own wife died about twenty-five years later I called Fay to commiserate about our loved ones' deaths. I said I'd stay in touch, but Fay's health has declined. When going through Atlanta I make sure to call her to ask to visit, but she always says she doesn't feel well enough to have me stop by.

Her health and memory are going quickly. "I'm getting old and I don't know nobody, and sometimes that's best," she told me during one call.

"I'm as old as you are and I'm doing OK," I chided.

"I think I worked a little harder than you did," she replied.

Chapter 8
Shipped Out

I left Majors Field in late 1944 when I transferred to the infantry. Learning to fly would somehow happen eventually, I figured, but it definitely wasn't going to happen in Greenville, Texas.

Following some infantry training in Camp Livingston, Louisiana, my group went by rail to Fort Meade, Maryland, for combat training. All they do in combat training is make you mad – mad enough to kill, your superiors hope. One guy in my unit didn't get the chance to use what he'd learned due to the benefit in combat training of using live ammunition. A few days after everyone survived crawling through a small field of barbed wire while machine-gun tracer bullets continuously fired eighteen inches above our heads, we lost that guy in an obstacle house. To simulate urban fighting, we had to work our way through a house rigged with guns to fire before we entered every room. He entered a room too soon, before the bullets had stopped, and became the first in our group to die.

I should note that the men who oversaw combat training never shipped out. They stayed put in Maryland because if any of us guys they'd made mad ever found them on a battlefield or in a trench, we'd forget who the real enemy was.

I was sent to Italy as an infantry replacement, but the fighting there was soon over. My name didn't come up to move to the front before the war ended, but other than that I was ready and prepared to be a replacement - and every day expected it. While in Italy, I did see some of the sights, such as the Leaning Tower of Pisa. "You know what that is?" someone asked me.

"Yeah, that's a silo that's about to fall over," I said. I'd never heard or read about Pisa or its tower.

I visited Rome, but didn't care much about what I was seeing because my education had been so lacking. I don't recall even hearing that the Pope lived in the Vatican or that the Vatican was its own city, much less located in Rome! But I do recall a performance staged by a USO troupe that came through because the main attraction was Frank Sinatra. A skinny New Jersey kid with a big voice, he had recently left the big band of Tommy Dorsey to start a solo singing career. The Italians went crazy because his family came from Italy. They threw such a fuss that the military agreed to hold two shows, one for the soldiers and one for the locals.

This was about the time that President Franklin Roosevelt died, in April 1945, soon after starting his fourth term in office. In early May, following the announcement of the end of the war in Europe, men with substantial combat records started to be sent to the states and some of us with little or no front-line experience were packed on ships headed for the Pacific war zone to fight the Japanese. My voyage to the Pacific started in June and lasted through August. We sailed through the Panama Canal and still had no clue where exactly we were headed. It was this boat trip that prompted me to decide never to take a cruise. Being infantry, we didn't have much to do except exercise and play cards – for weeks. Our ship was occasionally part of a formation of battleships and sub chasers. I say occasionally because we'd do maneuvers and then wake up the next morning with not one vessel in sight.

After the atomic bombs fell on Hiroshima and Nagasaki in early August 1945, we found out our mission. An announcement broadcast over the ship's intercom said we were to have been part of an invasion force on the Japanese mainland had the bombs not worked, and that our further status was unknown. A couple of days later – during which time we had hoped the boat would take us home – they said our destination was changed to the Philippines, where we were to rout out the Japanese soldiers who didn't know the war was over.

There were some freighters in the Filipino harbor where we docked in San Fernando City la Union, a beautiful area overlooking the ocean. In the area we were in there were units making up their time until they could get out of the service in a few months.

After a few weeks in the Philippines rounding up the Japanese, I, a sergeant, was assigned a work supervisor's job overseeing construction projects such as latrines and barracks. About half the crew consisted of Japanese prisoners. The other half was made up of Filipinos who were paid food and money.

For one job, I sent my corporal to get a load of workers from the detention facility to move a latrine and reset it. I had a jeep and could go from job to job, so I left my corporal to his duty. In my absence, one of the locals who was angry at the Japanese for overtaking his country persuaded the corporal to send one of the smaller prisoners around to the back side of a building where the Filipino could beat the stuffing out him. Pretty quickly, the Filipino came running back from around the building being chased by the Japanese prisoner. "Shoot him! Shoot him!" the Filipino yelled. That little Japanese prisoner surprised the Filipino with his Judo training, and the Filipino started getting his own ass beat.

Another incident during my time in the Philippines turned out to be humorous, but was nerve-wracking at the time. Military investigators from the Office of Strategic Services (OSS), the precursor to the Central Intelligence Agency, appeared at my unit headquarters one day and requested my commanding officer to locate and send me in for questioning. The post commander passed the duty to the young major in charge of my squadron, and the major approached me, frantically saying, "What are you into? Some kind of shit's going on, and there are some guys want me to take you to them. I don't want to, but this sounds serious!"

As puzzled as the major, I entered an office and sat uncomfortably on a chair while the OSS investigators took my fingerprints and launched very detailed and probing questions at me for what seemed like a long time: "Do you ever shoot craps? Where did you go when you left Camp Livingston, Louisiana? How did you travel? Did you gamble on the train?" Nothing they asked pointed to any behavior that was extremely bad. They concluded the interrogation by asking me to write my signature about fifty times. The investigators left the office for a minute, and returned to tell me I was free to go, "Sorry, you're not in trouble. We're looking for someone else who ended up with a money order during a crap game, changed the amount of money on it and signed your name in connection with cashing it."

I remember that we did have a crap game going on the troop transfer train from Camp Livingston to Memphis, en route to Fort Meade, Maryland. A serviceman carrying a government-issued money order was gambling with it. At one time in the game I held the money order because I had won a majority of its value. Eventually, it ended up in someone else's hands. The military investigators spent nearly a year trying to track down whoever misused it.

The young major in charge of my unit, who didn't want to take me in for questioning, treated me with respect and we worked well together. He would turn his duties over to me once in awhile so he could travel up in the nearby hills to a place called Bagio (now a resort) to go girl hunting. I was thinking about getting away to Bagio myself for a day in early December 1945 when he was preparing to return to the states. He talked of obtaining a civil service assignment back to the Philippines that would enable him to get a high government employment rating for being stationed there. The rating would give him a better income and retirement than he'd be eligible for from just being stationed in the states. "We could get you out and come back in the civil service," he suggested.

"If I get out of here and back home, I'm going to keep my ass there. If I get out I'm going to keep out," I said, not knowing or caring what civil service was.

In retrospect, if I'd entered the civil service, there's no telling how far I'd have advanced in life. It was a great opportunity that I just didn't understand. The major was probably somebody who dropped out of college and was now looking at a career he never would have considered before the war. It was an opportunity I missed because of my lack of understanding. If the major did return to the Philippines, I never did see him again.

For Christmas 1945, I was invited to Bagio by a black American veteran who had gone to the Philippines for the Spanish American War four decades earlier and stayed to raise a family. So far as I knew, he was the only African-American in the town. I had met him on one of my previous trips to Bagio, and he took a liking to me. He fixed quite a meal - we weren't eating dog! I say that because the primitive hill people along the road to Bagio, who lived in the bushes, would sit on the side of the trail with sticks through dogs turning them over fires, cooking them.

In fact, in Bagio you'd see dogs being held in the marketplace waiting to be purchased for food by the bush people, who'd walk into town wearing only g-strings around their privates and beaded bracelets covering their arms, carrying large bolo axes at their sides, capable of chopping trees as well as human heads. These natives existed wholly separate from the normal Filipino town folk we Americans dealt with on a regular basis. For a native wedding, the groom might need to present his in-laws with a human head to show his strength and bravery. Locals jokingly warned, "Don't stop on the way up there to Bagio; the hill people may behead you if they need a wedding gift."

Thankfully, I didn't have to wait long before leaving the Philippines for good. About two weeks after Christmas, I received orders to await transfer home. I finally shipped out in February 1946. We landed in San Francisco, and during the couple of days prior to being sent to Arkansas for discharge I visited an after-hours club and experienced my first and only time inhaling marijuana. The bar closed at midnight, so all after-hour activities happened downstairs. The smoke in the room was thick, so thick that a couple could be making out in a corner but you wouldn't know it. I didn't then and still don't know how to inhale, but you couldn't keep from breathing in while walking through the fog, I don't care what Bill Clinton says.

One cloudy-eyed individual offered me a drag on a joint, but I evidently didn't do it right because the guy said, "Give that shit back if you gonna waste it."

From San Francisco I started the long train ride to Camp Chaffee, Arkansas, where I received my honorable discharge on March 11, 1946 – three years, one month and two days after joining up.

Chapter 9
I Believe I Can Fly

Following my discharge, I stayed a few days with my sister Christine in Memphis, where I heard that my friend George Harris was also out of the service and staying at his family's home, about fifteen miles north of the city in a community known as Woodstock. George picked me up in his car, and we spent an afternoon in Orange Mound and on Beale Street before heading to the Harris farm for a little while. I mentioned that I would need to leave soon for Memphis to catch a bus to Ripley to see Aunt Lula and Uncle Fred. One of the Harrises said there was no need to go to Memphis; a bus could be flagged down at about 10 p.m. on the highway near what locals refer to as Harris Hill.

Still wearing my uniform, I flagged down a bus. The driver stopped, opened the door and told me I'd have to go to the back. I asked why.

"Because I said so."

When I said, "Well, I won't go to the back because I said so," he started charging down the steps at me, and I clubbed him. He wasn't necessarily a big guy, but big enough to think he could take care of me, and he may have been able to do it except for a negotiation technique I used. By the time he stood up I had already pulled out a Lugar pistol I'd taken from a Japanese officer while in the Philippines. (I had the papers authorizing me to bring it home, so I was not violating any laws in having it.) "I suspect you better get back on that bus," I told him.

So, I didn't get a bus ride. I walked to the house of one of George's nearby relatives and called George, who then drove me the roughly forty-five miles to Aunt Lula and Uncle Fred's home. The next day, following the telling of my bus story, Aunt Lula and Uncle Fred started growing concerned about the way my personality had changed while I was in the military. They questioned whether any one would come looking for me for retribution. Due to our differences in opinion, it turned out to be good that I hadn't planned to stay long with them (because there wasn't much to do in their community). In the several days I spent with them, I also visited my father in the community of Nutbush. Following the stay with Aunt Lula and Uncle Fred, I went to Memphis and spent my first three months or so of freedom living with my sister, Christine, and her husband, Willie "Buddy" Haywood.

Christine and Buddy were caring, religious people. Even though Christine and I did not spend many years close together physically, we kept space for each other in our hearts. She said when I was born some people speculated whether I was her child or our mother's. Christine was solidly built and worked in a dry cleaning business. Buddy also had a strong physique due to his years working construction jobs on highways and dams, though during and after the war he worked for a salvage company. They owned a house in a Memphis residential area called Binghampton that sprouted up after the war, an area that has grown cruddy in the years since. Christine and Buddy moved to Chicago around 1950.

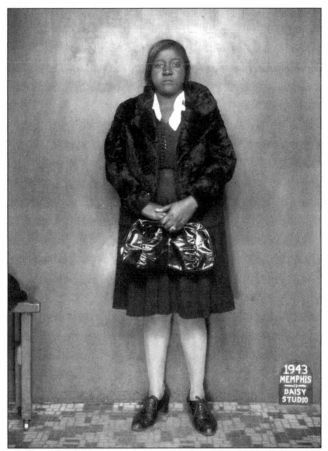

My sister, Christine Haywood, in 1943. Though we often lived far apart, our hearts beat closely together.

I wasn't sure what I wanted to do for my future. During my period of time with Christine and Buddy I had several thoughts: possibly starting a small business or going to college for dentistry or veterinary medicine. Not in any hurry to get anything permanent, I worked some odd jobs, one of which was driving a truck delivering groceries to rural village stores within a radius of twenty or thirty miles of Memphis. Some of my spare time was spent participating in activities with Buddy's Masonic Lodge, which I joined (I have since become inactive).

In the meantime, I kept reading newspapers and an item in one caught my eye. A flight school at a small airport in Memphis was advertising flight training through the GI Bill. Because flying hadn't left my mind, I decided to spend part of my GI Bill funds and get a private license, hoping that would fill my desire to pilot a plane. I figured that the sooner I could satisfy my urge, the sooner I could move on to finding an occupation that could help me meet my life goals: owning a business, living comfortably and raising a family. At this point, I saw flying as just a recreational activity.

On visiting the little airport whose advertisement I saw in the newspaper, I found I would not be welcomed into the flight school. One of the school's operators commented that a black pilot who had landed on his field to fuel a plane said that he was from a flight school in Nashville. The white man told me I would be better off finding that flight school in Nashville. Only months after I finished serving three years fighting for my country, I realized I was now home hoping for a social change that didn't exist.

My options being limited, I went to Nashville in May 1946, not knowing where this rumored flying school was. I found it and decided to attend, so over a short time I returned to Memphis, collected my belongings and transplanted to Nashville to enroll in the school, which boasted a thirty-day accelerated program.

Taylor Aeroservice had been started by James Taylor, formerly a civilian instructor for the Tuskegee flight program. He established the operation in coordination with Fisk University and employed other Tuskegee flight instructors who had been left out of work when that program was discontinued at the end of World War II. Instructors such as Cecil Ryan, Nathan Sams, Fred Witherspoon and Perry Young would contribute greatly to creating the pilot I was to become. My first instruction was given by Young, who would become the first African-American airline pilot, for the helicopter-flying New York Airways in the 1950s. Sams, who became one of the few blacks in the country to establish his own fixed-base operation at an airport, would send me on my first solo flight. Ryan, who became head of the aviation department at Tennessee State University, would provide me with my commercial certification a year later. Witherspoon, who became a businessman in Houston, would provide my training to be a flight instructor.

Taylor Aeroservice was situated on Cumberland Airfield, which was operated by Capitol Airways, a white business with whom the all-black Taylor Aeroservice had an arrangement. Taylor would fly or teach blacks, while Capitol took care of whites. Capitol occupied all the facilities on the north end of the field, and we were on the south end, housed in a modular building. Our planes had to be fueled and maintained by Capitol. We used some classrooms at Fisk University for ground school training.

Backed by the GI Bill, I was satisfied that I could enroll in this accelerated month-long summer program and obtain my private license, which was my goal. Jimmy Taylor helped me find a place to live that was also home to several other students in his program, the Price House, at 18th Street and Jefferson, across the street from the Fisk campus. The main floor was a drugstore operated by a Dr. Price; the remainder functioned as a rooming place for students of Taylor Aeroservice and the local medical school, Meharry Medical College.

At the end of my flight training, on July 31, 1947, I had to have a designated pilot examiner sign me off – the sort of examination I later did for about two thousand pilots over a 28-year period. There were just a limited number of people authorized to do that at that time, and only one who was black, C. Alfred Anderson. He was the designated chief of the flight program at the Tuskegee Institute, and had taken me on my first flight when I visited Tuskegee prior to joining the military. When I flew to Tuskegee to be certified for my private license in July 1946, it was my second time ever speaking to "Chief" Anderson, but I had found out a lot about him since our first meeting through becoming acquainted with a number of his colleagues and students. I had seen Chief also from afar when he had been to Nashville to see his old friends, so I wasn't intimidated, just glad to be with him. I satisfactorily passed the flight check.

As momentous as that occasion was, I more vividly remember a previous lesson during which Nathan Sams sent me up for my first flight alone. He gave me a lesson, and when we landed he said, "Now, it's your turn to go up by yourself." Those few words excited me because they made me realize that I was accomplishing what I had set out to do, and that maybe the better life I once dreamed about was around the corner.

Chapter 10
The Black Baron

While I was working toward my pilot's license, a fellow named Tom Hayes had bought a plane and was taking lessons at the airport during my last ten days of flight training. He read or heard of this plane that was so easy to fly it drove like a car, the two-seat Air Coupe.

Ready to pilot the Air Coupe bought by Tom Hayes, owner of the Birmingham Black Barons baseball team, 1946.

Hayes was a professional man. He ran a mortuary in Memphis, had controlling interest in a bank and insurance company, and owned the Birmingham Black Barons baseball team from 1939 to 1951 (during which time Willie Mays, Artie Wilson and Dan Bankhead played). He was among the most respected team owners in the Negro League, and history has remembered him for his team's success, his ability to promote and boost attendance, and his initiative in raising player salaries.

Tom was going to learn to fly, and he progressed to where he could get the plane up and down, but his lack of cross-country training and disinterest in enrolling at Fisk for ground school prevented him from following his ball team around. I had just obtained my license when he came to Cumberland and asked, "Can I get somebody who can go with me to fly this thing?" The other pilots at the airfield had families and didn't want to spend time away from them, so that left me to take the job. I was single with no attachments, so working for Tom Hayes served as a good time-filler until school started (I had decided to go to college). Chasing around the United States with him as his navigator and pilot, we'd travel to Chicago, Washington or Kansas City for games and return to Memphis. That was a lot of fun. In the years since I've run across people who were in the Negro League, though not with the Barons, and we talked about places where we were at the same time.

Tom was great to be around. In his upper forties, he was a senior person to me in age and status. The team traveled on a bus that Tom owned, and that was something in itself. He was a guy who could call somebody at our destination, and they'd have a suite ready at the hotel and also a room for me. Somebody would even meet us at the airport and take us. Tom was liberal and liked to have fun. I was received well because I was his pilot. Most people didn't have an airplane and just the fact I was his co-pilot gave me status. A hotel would have his suite all fixed up with the things that would make it the place to be, and Tom would always see that I had a good time, too. Girls always converge on athletes and an even more select group rises up to the management, and my proximity to Tom allowed me to enjoy some companionship. It was an exciting summer.

He and I kept in touch for a short while but eventually lost track of each other, and he's now been dead for some time. During a 2004 trip to Tennessee, I visited the Hayes and Son mortuary and took some pictures in memory of Tom. He and his brother, Taylor, inherited the business from their dad and they expanded it and it's outlived them.

The Memphis mortuary Black Barons owner Tom Hayes and his brother inherited is still operated by the family more than 100 years after its founding.

Chapter 11
Circle of Friends

After completing the summer flight program and piloting for Tom Hayes, I was still flirting with ideas for what to do with my life. Before I left Nashville, I decided I needed to enroll in college, so even though I took the job with Tom I intended to return when the fall term started the following month. The GI Bill helped me immensely; school would have been impossible without it. Many people who otherwise never would have found success have made it because of the GI Bill, which gives tuition and additional funds to help veterans eat and sleep, if they can find a cheap place to stay.

Even though no regular Fisk or Tennessee State students roomed at the Price House – just flight school and medical school students – before leaving Nashville with Tom Hayes I arranged with Dr. Price to continue renting through the school year. When I returned to start classes at Tennessee State, Alan Searcy, a good friend with whom I'd gone to school in Lauderdale County, had also entered TSU for the fall and was looking for a place to stay. I arranged for us to share my room in the Price House. Alan was one of those people who ended up not living a long life, so I've grown glad that our relationship was strengthened by rooming together.

There were some other people I met or reconnected with through Price House, Tennessee State and Taylor Aeroservice who became long-lasting friends, including George Jones, Ted Davidson, Perry Beatles, Zanas Hargrove, Clarence Wilson, John Cashin, Virgil Boston, Samuel Lee and Nesbit Austin, to name a few.

Starting the first Saturday evening of the month, payday weekend, some of us would gather in Price House and play poker straight through to Monday morning – until somebody's girlfriend would call and raise hell and he had to leave. Alan Searcy's then girlfriend, later his wife, Dorothy, called one time wanting to talk to Alan, but John Halliburton, who did not play poker, answered the phone. Alan told him to tell Dorothy he wasn't there, so John returned to the phone and told Dorothy, "Alan said to tell you he wasn't here." Dorothy later said she thought she'd never be able to forgive Alan for his lie, but that she'd always remember John for his honesty.

George Jones was an exciting guy because he knew the town and had connections. His parents owned the Top Hat Club, which was the most noted black-owned nightspot in Nashville at that time, and it was there that I met him.

He would bartend occasionally, and would attract a number of female customers. He sometimes needed help pushing women away. Although I was dating the woman who would become my wife and would double date with George and whomever he was seeing, he and I occasionally went out in his car for fun and competed to get somebody else's girls. George and I later moved to Wichita, Kansas, together, bought houses side by side and raised families.

John Cashin and I became good friends while he lived at Price House as a pre-med student. John became very interested in aviation and, as with George, I convinced him to enroll in flying lessons, and after he became a successful dentist in Huntsville, Alabama, he bought his own plane. In 1959, John received national attention for being the first black to run for governor of Alabama. He's now retired, with homes in Huntsville and Washington, D.C.

It was Samuel Lee, though, who joined me in my first college business venture. Not long into my fall enrollment, I had an idea. Students were walking around with nothing to do in their spare time, and I'd see others riding their bicycles. The kids who came to Nashville from out of town didn't have bicycles and very few had cars. In the post-World War II years not many young people, college bound or not, could afford automobiles.

Samuel Lee helped me run the Jefferson St. Cycle Co. in Nashville. He later became the last principal of Lauderdale County Training School.

Hoping to cash in on a demand that hadn't yet been identified, I opened a bicycle rental shop. I found an ideal location on Jefferson Street between Fisk University and Tennessee State, about a mile from each, and named the operation the Jefferson Street Cycle Co.: "Don't Hike, Rent a Bike" was the business motto. I bought a couple bicycles, and fixed up and painted them to look new, and I opened up a rental place with those two bikes and business took off. With a need for some financial assistance and help operating the business, I brought Samuel on as a partner. People lined up to wait for renters to bring bikes back. We charged about fifty cents an hour or a dollar for three hours. Word spread that I was interested in used bicycles, and I became pretty good at fixing them and trained Samuel to tear down the bikes, strip paint, paint the frames, install new bearings. Using spare parts we had people riding what looked to be new bicycles, and we started advertising.

The front and back of the business card for the bicycle rental shop I operated while enrolled at Tennessee State University. The shop was strategically located mid-way between Tennessee State and Fisk University to accommodate students of both institutions.

The idea caught on so much that a guy on the east side of Fisk took my idea and bought a fleet of brand new bicycles. It didn't drive me out of business, due to my prime location, but it showed that my idea was a good business venture. The noteworthy part about starting school at Tennessee State was that I went there with a plan for my future. I thought I would do two years of college and then transfer to the veterinary school at the Tuskegee Institute; flying would just be a fun thing to do on weekends.

Splitting my time between school and the bike shop, any opportunity when I had some extra money would be used to rent an airplane. News of my flying circulated around campus, and girls thought that was pretty neat. I'd take one girl out flying and she'd go back and tell her friends, and it'd make it pretty easy to pick up another one. That made me a very popular freshman at school, even though I didn't own a car. I'd fly on weekends or evenings, and that would serve two purposes: satisfying the lifelong desire I had to fly airplanes and giving me additional hours of experience that could be used to upgrade my flight rating, though I didn't realize until later how much of an asset that was. At the time I thought I was just going to college and flying for the hell of it. Building experience wasn't as important as feeling that I was doing what I felt like I wanted to do, fly.

Occasionally I would rent an airplane and fly with some of my fellow Nashville students to where I grew up in the western part of the state. Some of my pals, such as Samuel Lee and Alan Searcy, were from the same area. They'd like to hook up with me and pay a bit of the cost. It worked out conveniently that I was acquainted with an airplane owner in Nashville who would let me use his aircraft on weekends for less than the cost of renting from a flight service – the cost of fuel plus a small fee.

I would fly once or twice a month to West Tennessee, landing in the pasture near where my Aunt Lula and Uncle Fred lived on a small farm. There was no airport, but having grown up there I knew the lay of the land and where I could touch down. For one trip in the fall of 1947 on which I had driven to Lauderdale County, I went hunting with some friends outside Henning. They mentioned that they were disappointed I hadn't flown; they all wanted rides to fly over a relative or girlfriend's house so they could go back and say they flew over.

There was a grass field at Henning owned by a white guy who put a mobile home there and started a flight-training business. I had been surprised to find that it was located there, but there were then and are now a lot of small grass airports around. After our hunt we went out to this place and the operator was very hesitant about even talking to me about renting an airplane, because I looked fairly ragged, having spent the day walking through the woods with a gun. But he gathered I knew how to fly and wasn't just some guy from the cotton patch. He said he'd have to go up with me for a trial flight, which I understood was standard procedure for renting a plane. When we came back he let me take my friends up and told me anytime I wanted to rent a plane, just come out. That field became a regular spot for me to land and it was handy, but there was no fuel there. Whenever I went there I had to make sure I had enough gas to return to Jackson to get fuel enough to get to Nashville.

A year or so later, after using that field and becoming familiar with the man who owned it, I had driven down by myself and was out bird hunting again with another group of guys. We were close to Henning and we started talking about flying, so I offered. We went to the mobile home and there were a couple of white boys standing around in jeans. I asked where the man was who owned the place. "Oh, he's down in Memphis. Did you want him to take you up in the airplane?"

"Oh, nope, nooo way," I said, seeing a chance to fool them that I was afraid of flying. I had already earned my commercial license and was flying shows and doing aerobatics by this time.

The other guys were waiting at the car unaware of the conversation. I suggested we go take a look at the plane, which was the same type I was doing an air-show act with. "You sit in the back, I'll sit in front," the boy said, thinking I was scared to death to go flying.

"How do you get in this thing?" I asked. I got in and said, "Well I'm in here now so I'll let one of you take me up." I was getting the feel of what was going on.

They looked at each other and one said, "Well, if we go up, we're going to do some stunts. You want to go?"

"I'm already here!" I said.

They whispered between themselves, apparently deciding who would pilot. One of them got in, and I watched his piloting style as he took the aircraft into the air. I was already an instructor and could tell he was an early student. My friends on the ground probably thought he was going to see if I could fly, the way the operator had done when I rented previously. While flying around the airport, he'd rapidly pull back on the stick and then push forward, attempting to frighten me. I figured stalls would be the limit of what he'd been taught, putting the plane into temporary free fall. He pulled up and looked like he was going to do a stall but didn't quite want to. I thought to myself, "The next time I'm going to hold on and give you a test."

He got about brave enough to get the nose up to stall attitude, and though my hands indicated that I was holding on for dear life, I put my leg in front of the stick so that he couldn't move it forward, and the plane stalled and dropped off. We went upside down, and this guy's hands went into the air. Then I grabbed the stick and took him for a real ride. I rolled that plane, looped it and did a spin down to the end of the runway and landed and taxied up to the trailer.

In the meantime, the man who owned the plane showed up and started going berserk while we were in the air. When I taxied the plane up and stopped, this kid got out and wobbled over to the trailer and spewed out everything but his guts. The boss asked the people on the ground, "Why didn't someone tell me he was up there with a flight instructor?"

I told him what happened, "He was going to take me up and scare the hell out of me."

"I'm glad you did it!" the man said. "I'm glad it happened to him."

—*Reflections*—

My Price House friends hosted a wedding dinner for Augusta Fields and me at Nashville's Top Hat Club.

Chapter 12
Augusta

A running joke among my friends is that I won Augusta Fields, the woman who would become my wife, in a poker game.

Augusta Fields in 1943. We met at Tennessee State University three years later, and married in 1948.

I was initially introduced to her by Nesbit Austin during my thirty days in flight school. Nesbit, who was dating Augusta at the time, had lived in an adjoining county, Tipton, during high school when I first met him and he had enrolled in Tennessee State after leaving the military. We might have crossed paths in a park near the university. Neither of us knew anyone else well at all, so we renewed our acquaintance. "You know, those girls at Tennessee State are awfully good looking," Nesbit said one day. "My girl has a friend I could set you up with. How about we do a double-date some night? Both these girls are beautiful and were star players on their high school's basketball team at Summerville, Tennessee."

We ended up double-dating a couple of times before I graduated from Taylor Aeroservice, and when I returned to Tennessee State, Nesbit and I continued double-dating those girls, though not on a serious basis.

Then came a fateful poker game.

Kidding each other about women during the game, I asked Nesbit if he was serious about Augusta, whose high cheekbones and large eyes appealed to me, and if he'd mind some competition. "I like competition," he said. "Give it your best shot!" He ended up losing his money in that game, and when his girlfriend called him to go out, he couldn't afford to. That's when I moved in. Augusta and I started dating on a regular basis.

Like me, Augusta had not been raised by her mother. Born July 12, 1927, she was reared by her grandmother in rural Haywood County, Tennessee, which adjoined Lauderdale County's east side. Though poor, Augusta was very intelligent and athletic. While in high school she played basketball and was valedictorian of her senior class. She was in her sophomore year of college by the time we met, planning to become a home economics teacher. Cooking and sewing were activities Augusta excelled at, and she eventually took up upholstering furniture as a hobby.

After roughly a year together, on December 18, 1947, Augusta and I had our first serious clash. We had some very strong words while on a double-date with Ted Davidson, and we split. I don't remember how it all came about, but the situation became very disagreeable. Maybe part of it was that I was still dating other girls besides Augusta, and she was jealous about the ones who went flying with me.

My gang worked the disagreement out. The guys had grown close to Augusta and liked her. I think she and I were swamped with people determined we should put our conflict behind us. She left Nashville for Christmas break, but returned to school in January, and by February we were back together.

Augusta and I always remembered the date of our fight, December 18, because we married exactly a year later. We liked to say we finished 1947 with a breakup and finished '48 with a big makeup.

There wasn't much money to put into a celebration for our union, but we had a fine time. Her girlfriends threw her a little party, and my crew threw me one. Samuel Lee says I messed up the gang by being the first one married, but those guys sure supported me in doing it. For my party, Clarence Wilson, who had been a Navy cook, and Alan Searcy, who was also ex-Navy personnel, put aside their running debate over who was the better chef and teamed up to fix a steak dinner. Along with that we had booze and poker, and no women involved for the evening.

Out of that party came a running joke amongst ourselves. After we finished eating and were going around the table telling big lies, Ted Davidson, who was a small guy, said, "You know what this reminds me of? Well, the animals had a big dinner in the woods, and the lion raised up after he was through eating and said, 'Ugliest one around this table is going to have to wash the dishes.' The monkey looks at the ape and says, 'I may have to wash 'em but you're going to have to dry 'em!'"

It was a simple house wedding, very simple. Augusta made her own dress and I wore a regular dress suit. In attendance were Aunt Lula and one of my cousins, my guys and the girls Augusta associated with at Tennessee State. The climax came when George Jones arranged for a post-wedding reception at his parents' Top Hat nightclub. The next day Augusta and I just settled in, resumed life as usual, no honeymoon or long travel. Our marriage didn't seem to suffer from that omission, though; Augusta and I were committed to each other for forty-nine years.

—Reflections—

Wedding portrait of my wife, Augusta.

Chapter 13
Getting Focused

When I enrolled at Tennessee State, my first plan was to be a veterinarian. Enrolled in the agriculture program, I don't know how much love I had for animals, but being raised on a farm and being around animals made me figure it was something I could do, but, I was proved wrong.

Due to flight hours I was accumulating on weekends and other odd times, I was able to gain my commercial piloting license and serve as a charter pilot. The other pilots at Taylor's Aeroservice were all married and liked to be home, which left me to do flights to Chicago or Louisville overnight.

There's one story told about me that I have to mention because it's been published before and told many times. During 1948 one of my agriculture projects consisted of raising chickens. I had a trip for which I was supposed to go and come right back during the week because I was in class. We were weathered in and didn't return for two days. The story goes that when I got back, the chickens I was looking after had died.

Actually, the chickens didn't die, but my supervisor said they could have. "Gooch, you are going to have to make up your mind," he said. "You can't keep dividing your time between my class and flying. If you want to make it in life, you have to decide. I'm not telling you which to do; just make up your mind."

I decided I was sick of taking care of chickens. On March 10, 1948, I earned my commercial pilot license and on June 18 received my flight instructor certification. With my credentials growing, I phased out the bicycle shop and soon became an instructor with Taylor Aeroservice.

At about that time, several of my friends who were taking classes at Taylor Aeroservice nearly died in a plane crash. Ted Davidson, one of my early students who also lived in Price House, Harry Bittle and Zanas Hargrove were flying to Wilburforce University in Ohio to get some supplemental ground school instruction. When Taylor Aeroservice students failed written tests they would be sent to Wilburforce for a weekend cram session with Louis Jackson, who had been in charge of the ground school at Moton Airfield.

Louis Jackson, head of the cadet flight training program at Tuskegee, Alabama's Moton Field during World War II, and his wife. The men who graduated the program became known as the Tuskegee Airmen, one of the elite groups in African-American history.

Students who took the test and failed at Taylor's had to wait about 90 days before taking it again unless a certified ground school instructor authorized a retake sooner. Louis could put students through some training that would help. Guys would spend a weekend cramming at Wilburforce, return and retake the test, often successfully. Louis knew what he was doing and was very aggressive; he later was responsible for building the first car plane. Ted, Harry and Zanas ran into some bad weather that caused them to crash and get badly hurt. Almost immediately after receiving news of the accident, I high-tailed it to the hospital where they were near Wilburforce. While walking down the hall to where the nurse had pointed me, I could hear Ted tell the doctor, "I don't care how you say I am, long as you get me back to flying airplanes!"

Though Harry and Zanas would recover and finish their flight certifications, Ted was about half gone. He came out with so much damage that he wouldn't be able to get his commercial license, mostly due to his legs getting messed up – but he was upset and went into the aircraft mechanic program at Tennessee State. He ended up in California and got assigned to a major secret project – an Air Force spy plane, the Blackbird. It was years before anyone could talk about it; it flew so high it was undetectable, and could observe things all over the world.

Ted and I would lose and regain contact over the years, but we had rekindled our friendship by the time he died in January 2004. There's a Blackbird on exhibition at the Cosmosphere space museum in Hutchinson, Kansas, about an hour from Wichita, and whenever I see it I remember Ted Davidson.

When I started flying full time I engaged in a lot of weekend barnstorming. I was limited in the number of hours I could fly as an instructor due to Civil Aeronautics Administration (now FAA) regulations, but I had no limit to the hours I could fly on my own time.

My first class of flight students at Nashville's Cumberland Airfield around 1948.

An air troupe I hooked up with would perform at picnics and celebrations on weekends in spring and summer. One job I did involved taking people up for airplane rides. The event organizers picked out a dead-end road some-where near a new highway. The road had been closed when the highway was put in, but there was a lone farmhouse near the dead-end. It was an ideal location to land my four-place Stinson Voyager, about a half mile from the function. The customers would come down the road and wait to go on a ride, and I'd fly them around and land on this strip. I didn't know that no one had asked the folks in the house for their approval to use the road.

We'd been using most of the length of this road to take off, and at one point I was carrying a pretty heavy load. The more weight we had, the more space we'd need to take off. I started my takeoff run down the road and about the time the tail came off the ground a car pulled out of the driveway at the end of the road and right into my path. At this time I was almost eyeball to eyeball with the car's driver. I popped one notch of flap, and with a sudden liftoff I almost rolled the wheels on the top of that car. The passengers didn't understand how close we'd come to a crash.

Was I scared? Ask my laundry lady.

Also during that time I associated with another weekend air show crew, doing an act that was known as the runaway plane – so called because a pilot disguised as a spectator takes off in the plane and scares the audience. It was very impressive when I did it, not that others didn't do it then and still do it today, but my act was so exciting because everybody was sure that the person in that plane couldn't fly.

Staging the act required a plane to be parked somewhere visible to the air show audience, and required me to mingle with the crowd as a spectator. I'd get out there before the show, get my plane in when no one was around and get out with my blue bib overalls and straw hat, with a pipe in my mouth and a liquor bottle filled with water in my back pocket. When the show started, I would appear in the crowd and start moving around, so everybody could observe me there acting like I wished I hadn't shown up. In this way, everyone became aware of my presence yet they would be dissuaded from visiting with me. During the flying acts, I'd amble over to my Piper Cub and the show announcer would say, "Hey, who's that over by that airplane? He ain't supposed to be out there!"

He'd work on getting everybody's attention focused on what was happening, and then ask a pilot to get me away from the plane. I'd then ask the pilot, "Where's the guy who's giving airplane rides?"

"We ain't giving rides now; wait until the show's over!" the announcer would say.

The pilot would yell to the announcer, "He won't wait, he says he wants to go now," to which the announcer would respond, "Go take that guy up so we can get him out of here. And don't be long; that plane is low on gas."

The air shows in which I flew also featured sky divers such as Red Didget, who had a unique parachuting method.

The pilot would help me get into the Piper Cub's back seat, where I would normally sit to fly anyway, and he would get in the front.

We'd taxi to the end of the runway to takeoff position, and the pilot would get out to check the rear wheel.

"He's looking at the tail wheel. Something must be wrong with it," the announcer would say frantically. I would hit the gas to start the airplane moving.

"Hey, get that guy!" the announcer would yell as the pilot came running after the plane. I would let up on the gas so he could catch up a bit and then accelerate and take off.

Of course, I would fly around, take the throttle down, swoop low and yell, "I don't know how to fly!" Bill Sweet, the show organizer, would make a big production out of that, partly due to his drinking half a six-pack of beer by the time I started my act.

"Isn't there a book in there, *Learn How to Fly*? You got a book in there!" And I'd hold up the book and let it fly out the window.

"Oh, no, the book's flown out the window? How's he going to fly that thing?"

On one occasion in fall 1948 in Bowling Green, Kentucky, Augusta came along to see me perform in the show. As I flew around, she sat near the announcer.

"Well, I hope he stays away from here because he's going to run out of gas and crash the thing, and I don't want him to crash into the crowd!" Bill Sweet yelled throwing the crowd into an uproar. A patrolman came running up to the announcing area in his car, "Do you think we'd be better off shooting him down so he doesn't crash into the crowd?"

"Oh, NO!" Augusta gasped.

Bill whispered to him, "Man, it's just part of the act!"

After I'd make two or three passes I'd climb up and cut the engine, at which point the announcer would alert the audience I had run out of gas. I'd then do a couple of loops and a spin, and finally maneuver down to landing position and roll up to the crowd on one wheel and then put the plane down. I'd get out of the plane and the announcer would say, "Get that guy!" I'd run, and the audience would always catch me.

"Ladies and gentlemen: Rip Gooch!" Bill would introduce me. "All the way from Tennessee State!"

Audiences did not want to believe I was flying that airplane. You didn't find anybody colored around airports doing anything but washing airplanes. Air shows also attracted a lot more whites than blacks.

Other people performed the runaway plane act, but Bill Sweet liked me because he could really catch his audiences off guard, and spook them.

—*Reflections*—

Though air shows have changed in the decades since I performed the runaway plane act, their spirit remains intact at such events as Operation Skyhook, shown here at Pine Bluff, Arkansas, in 2003.

Chapter 14
A Short Detour

By early 1949, the civilian aviation industry was moving into a slump. Small-plane manufacturers who had kept busy making training aircraft for the military during World War II and then sold aircraft to civilian flight training schools after the war were finding their well running dry. Flight schools such as Jim Taylor's Aeroservice couldn't buy planes because their numbers of students were dwindling. It was one big trickle-down effect.

The men who had returned from war and used GI Bill money to learn to fly were finding that most piloting jobs – for airlines and corporations – had been taken by guys who already had piloting experience in the war. Additionally, men would drop out of flight school and prospective students wouldn't even attend because they decided to use their GI Bill money to enter trade schools or colleges that would prepare them for careers with a future. Aside from GI Bill funding, many people who would have wanted to fly couldn't afford to because they were busy starting families and putting their lives back together on the homefront.

The civilian aviation industry would not bounce back until the 1950s, when the World War II veterans had settled into their jobs and communities and decided they had disposable income to invest in aviation as a hobby. A significant group of these flight enthusiasts consisted of doctors.

Until then the situation was sad, particularly for blacks, because the only real piloting jobs involved teaching other blacks how to be flight instructors. And one can only produce so many flight instructors before there are no more students, especially in the black community where interest in flying was limited to start with.

Even Tuskegee Airmen who had left the military were excluded from being hired to fly airline or corporate aircraft due to discrimination. Only a handful of exceptions found flying jobs. When the Korean War started in 1950, a few African-Americans were hired as civilian instructors for the military, including Leroy Eley, Charles Smallwood, Joe Bennett and former Tuskegee instructors Sherman Rose and Milton Crenshaw, who had closed his flight training operation in Little Rock due to lack of business. A handful of other blacks were hired for non-flying federal aviation jobs such as air-traffic controlling and inspecting: Luke Weathers, Span Watson, Bill Broadwaters, Roscoe Draper and a few others.

More than 100,000 flight hours, from left: Leroy Eley Sr., me, Joe Bennett, Roscoe Draper and Milton Crenshaw.

Airline piloting jobs for blacks would not materialize in quantity until the early 1970s when the government initiated a class-action lawsuit against United Airlines. The ball started rolling in 1973 when the Tuskegee Airmen incorporated themselves as a legally recognized organization. At that time only about five African-Americans had been employed as airline pilots, including Perry Young with New York Airways, Jim Tillman with American Airlines and Marlon Green with Continental; Argus Martin was actually the first African-American hired as a commercial pilot, but that was in the Caribbean. Government representatives attended a Tuskegee Airmen meeting and asked why nearly none of the members worked for the airlines and whether any would still be eligible for employment. The original Tuskegee Airmen were not eligible for hire because they were reaching retirement age, but they provided the government with names of black pilots who had applied to work for the airlines and been brushed off. About ten pilots joined the class-action lawsuit against United, and though some dropped out, the courts found in favor of the pilots. The settlement allowed the pilots to work for United and receive employment credit back to the time they first applied to work for the airline. The lead pilot in the lawsuit, Jim Edwards, for instance, received time eligibility going back to 1966; he retired from United in the 1990s. In the wake of the ruling, all the other airlines started hiring African-Americans so as to avoid also being sued. Among the pilots hired in this period was the first black female airline pilot, Jill Brown with Continental. Unfortunately, she was cut from the airline during her probation period, likely because she was often interrupted in her duties by media attention. Another early female airline flight crew member, Shirley Tyus, was promoted from flight attendant to flight engineer and eventually pilot. She is still flying. Both women had gained piloting proficiency with the same flight operation in North Carolina, Wheeler Airline.

In the late 1940s, no progress was on the horizon, and Jimmy Taylor decided to close his Aeroservice in Nashville and move to Texas to help his wife run a mortuary her parents owned. During Aeroservice's last months, I was one of three instructors. Cecil Ryan left first to head the aviation department at Tennessee State University. Shortly thereafter Fred Witherspoon moved to Texas, took a job with the U.S. Postal Service and never flew again. At the very end, Aeroservice was left with just Jimmy and me.

The business had a few students who had not completed flight training – my friends George Jones, Buddy House, Walton Alexander and William "Tiny" Davis – and I made an agreement with Jimmy to finish them up as he was leaving. So I could do it, Jimmy sold me a Piper J3 in which I had received some of my flight training, cost: $672.

With the total closure of Taylor's Aeroservice and limited flying prospects, I had to look for another means of employment. With a wife to support (Augusta was in her last year of student teaching), I decided to find a job that could earn me more money than flying could. I didn't give up on flying, but I didn't have any luck with it, either. Through some well-placed contacts, I finagled a job as an appliance salesman for the Nashville-based McKissack Brothers construction firm, which had decided to sell appliances because the post-World War II demand was so high. The brothers were the sons of the owners of the McKissack and McKissack architecture and engineering business that had most notably built the air base at Tuskegee, Alabama – the largest federal contract given to a black-owned company up to 1942.

My work selling appliances would be brief – done while I was trying to finish teaching the Aeroservice students – but the sales training I received would stay with me for decades.

After a couple of months, when my flight students fizzled out, the McKissacks transferred me from selling appliances to being a labor foreman, a job I'd hold for the next year. This allowed me to make money on salary rather than commission.

One doesn't have to know how to build a house to be a labor foreman; one just has to have the intelligence to keep things moving – carpenters here, plumbers there, etc. I learned a little bit from working for the McKissacks, but a lot of what I did was traced back to my work in the Philippines, moving people from job to job. Coincidentally, my military discharge papers had noted that I would make a great construction foreman.

During my time with the McKissacks, we worked on post-war government housing projects, the renovation of the National Baptist Hotel and Bath House in Hot Springs, Arkansas, and construction of a business school in Birmingham for black millionaire A.G. Gaston.

Working on the hotel brought back some memories because I'd stayed there with Black Barons baseball team owner Tom Hayes. The red-brick building was one of the plush marvels of its day, with four stories covering ten acres and housing a 75-room hotel, a 100-bed hospital and nurse training school, a bank, a printing plant, offices and a 2,500-seat auditorium. Though still standing and listed on the National Register of Historic Places, the National Baptist Hotel and Bath House is now dilapidated and boarded up.

As for A.G. Gaston, whom I would eventually get to know a little bit, a few years after he returned from service in World War I he used $500 to start the Birmingham-based Booker T. Washington Insurance Company, the cornerstone of what would be a $130 million empire that included, among other interests, mortuaries, media outlets, a bank, a bottling plant and a construction company (which Gaston started at age 94). His Booker T. Washington Business College served to instill economic sense in young African-Americans who, due to Jim Crow America, might never have otherwise learned how to make money through the principles of hard work, dependability, courtesy, honesty and thrift – qualities Gaston constantly espoused.

One thing I observed while working for the McKissacks was that the small number of minority-owned businesses that were succeeding in their growth utilized other minority businesses when they needed things done. Minorities knew they were not getting an opportunity to be competitive in the open market with majority companies, so they had to help each other.

Like my sales training, this knowledge would prove useful in the years to come.

Chapter 15
Capitol Airways

Aside from the construction business, I kept busy giving flight lessons and doing air shows, or at least contacting people trying to get those opportunities. Occasional weekends were spent with my gang of friends playing poker. Many evenings, though, I spent with Augusta taking care of our new addition, Camellia Ann Gooch, who was born March 21, 1950. Another reason Augusta and I didn't venture out much around town was that we didn't have the means to do so. My efforts to try to earn more money met racial barriers.

My first child, Camellia Ann Gooch, in front of the Gooch family apartment at 510 Eighth Avenue South in Nashville.

In one instance, toward the end of my time with Taylor's Aeroservice, some white pilots with Capitol Airways at Cumberland Airfield recommended that I sign up to fly with the Tennessee Air National Guard. The pay would make for a good supplemental income and the aircraft available to us would be cutting edge and allow for further flight certification, they said. When I went in to the Guard office to discuss the matter, the receptionist had a difficult time understanding that I could even fly airplanes. She handed me papers to fill out, which I did. I left briefly but returned to ask how long she thought it would be before someone contacted me. As I opened the door I saw her tearing some papers, and I was sure she was tearing up the ones I had just filled out.

Indeed, I'm still waiting to hear from the Tennessee Air National Guard.

In 1951, while I actively pursued getting a full-time piloting job with Capitol Airways, which was expanding into charter work, I ran into the same obstacle. By that time Capitol had left Cumberland Airfield to become the fixed-base operation at Berry Field, the home of Nashville's busiest airport, eventually Nashville International. As the fixed-base operation, Capitol would sell and service airplanes and take care of people flying in and through, the same things it did at Cumberland Field, where I had become familiar with owners Jesse Stallings and Henry Cannon.

Stallings, the primary partner, had piloted for American Airlines and the U.S. Army and held the record for the first non-stop trans-Atlantic cargo flight from Scotland to New York. Upon moving to Berry Field in 1949, he purchased a DC-3 (expanded in a few years to a fleet of 40 transport planes) and chartered for the Western Kentucky State College basketball team and performers from the Grand Ole Opry.

Cannon, also a former Army pilot, was even more tightly connected to the Opry – his wife was Minnie Pearl! She called him Hezzie, the name of the imaginary beau she talked about in her comedy routines.

Even though Taylor's Aeroservice and Capitol Airways had maintained separate but unequal facilities at Cumberland Field, we had to buy fuel from them and they knew who we were. Neither group made it appear it was part of the other's organization.

When I called on Stallings at Berry Field, I knew Capitol needed pilots – each of his planes required two. Jess went back and forth without giving me a real answer about letting me fly for him. He finally said, "I can give you a job helping out in the shop, and then we'll see if we can come up with something." I quit the McKissack Brothers for temporary work cleaning up parts in the shop, cleaning up airplanes and getting aircraft ready for trips. Eventually, Jess came up with an idea to employ me through his connection to the Grand Ole Opry.

The Opry was in its heyday, with Hank Williams' "Your Cheatin' Heart" and Little Jimmy Dickens' "Tater don't taste good when chicken's on the plate." The Opry would occasionally be contracted to perform somewhere by Hadacol, a company that produced what was basically a poor-grade whiskey that could "cure" everything. Appearances by the Hadacol Caravan Medicine Show, as it was billed, always resulted in Hadacol being sold by the truckload. To make sure everyone within the area of the performance knew the caravan was there, Hadacol paid for a small plane to fly around dragging a banner –

and that was the only flying job I obtained courtesy of Jesse Stallings.

I believe to this day that Jess was serious in his thinking about the uselessness of segregation, but he finally told me I wasn't going to get a job: "When a crew flies into different locations and has to be somewhere overnight, I can have my crew put up at a place all together – but I couldn't mix you with the crew because you couldn't stay there," he said.

Stallings couldn't place me on his crew at that key time, right before an expansion period that would make Capitol Airways one of the foremost charter airplane operations in the world. At one point in the 1960s Capitol was given exclusive rights to ship cargo for Lufthansa and Air France. As a contract carrier for the U.S. military (troops and whatever else), Capitol would post a ninety-eight percent on-time and reliability rate. Though Capitol went out of business in the early 1980s, it had an admirable run and I'm still kind of disappointed I wasn't part of it.

—Reflections—

My peers in the 1940s Nashville aviation community would never have imagined an aircraft such as the Virgin Atlantic GlobalFlyer, used by billionaire Steve Fossett in 2005 to set a record for the first solo, non-stop around-the-world flight. I visited the plane's base in Salina, Kansas, later that year.

Chapter 16
The Wild Man

Though I did not fly for Capitol Airways, I was able to earn extra money flying odd jobs for a young man who was a story by himself.

Neil Cargile grew up well-to-do in Nashville, the son of the president and general manager of a company that made home heaters, cooking ranges and, during World War II, bombs and barracks heaters. I first met him at Cumberland Airfield when he started flying lessons with Capitol while still in his early high school days.

Shortly after he was certified for solo flying, Capitol discovered he had found a grass pasture south of the city where a friend was meeting him and going up for rides. That was his first problem with Capitol, which after a few incidents decided it wasn't going to be bothered with him, so Neil bought himself his own airplane.

And another airplane.

And another.

Using military surplus aircraft parts, he also rebuilt a plane in his yard – at age sixteen. He was a daredevil, too, on one occasion supposedly buzzing his father on a local golf course. He probably did, because he later buzzed a college in nearby Murfreesboro. Neil had just bought a BT-13 like we had at Greenville, Texas, because he wanted a big, round engine that made a lot of noise. After buzzing the school, he returned to Berry Field, parked the plane and left.

Word immediately spread about the incident, and Capitol started fielding calls from police wanting to know who had this plane that was buzzing the college. No one else around Nashville had a plane like that BT-13, so that narrowed the search significantly. A few hours later, the sheriff came out with log chains and put them around Neil's plane to tie it down.

Everybody was wondering when the police were going to pick up Neil Cargile. He disappeared and for a long time no one knew what happened to him. Months passed.

Finally, it leaked that he had joined the Navy and gone to Navy flight school. Soon thereafter, the people at Berry Airfield were out looking around and listening to the tower, when a request was radioed in for a Navy plane to make a low high-speed pass and landing.

The tower responded that it didn't understand the request for a high-speed pass of Berry Fi – Whhooom! – "What was it that passed over?" A Navy fighter went around, came back over and was cleared to land. It rolled up the strip and parked, and who got out of the plane but Neil Cargile. The next we heard of him was that he was no longer in the Navy.

When he returned for good, Neil employed me to do some crop dusting. He had started buying up all the surplus planes he could find and outfitting them for aero-application, as we called dusting. For a Stearman PT-17 biplane he picked up in Jackson, Tennessee, he installed a BT-13 Pratt-Whitney 450 engine as part of his spray-plane conversion. Neil would often buy these planes wherever he could, sight unseen, such as a Stearman he bought in Pontiac, Michigan, north of Detroit. Neil was very adventurous and had a lot of money at his disposal, but he was tight with how he spent it. "I've bought an airplane in Michigan and need it brought to Jackson. I'll give you $150 to get it down here," he told me, "but, you've got to get there the least expensive way you can, put gas in it and fly it back; what money's left is yours."

I went up by bus, and this open-cockpit Stearman biplane was buried in a snow bank. The plane's seller and I dug it out and moved it into the hangar to heat up. The next morning the plane was warm enough to start and head south, but still wasn't terribly warm. I wore a heavy fur-lined flight suit because I knew the weather was going to be cold, but I didn't know it was going to be that cold. I headed south, and had a little windshield that sent the air over me, so I could sit under the cold air stream. I would raise up once in a while to look around. Finally, I reached Richmond, Indiana, and landed on a grass airfield and taxied up to the operation building for gas. I started to get out but couldn't because my legs weren't moving. I sat there and the caretaker came over. "I can't get up," I told him, my legs numb and stiff. Some guys came over and tried to help out, and worked my legs so I could move. They had a kerosene or oil burning heater in the airport building, and they stretched me out on a bench and worked my limbs to stimulate circulation. The only time in the 60 years I've been flying that I ever took off or landed within hours of a drink of alcohol was at Richmond. One ol' boy asked, "You going to fly outta here in that airplane?"

"If I can get back in it."

"What you ought to have is a good drink of bourbon, and I just happen to have one out there in my pickup." This guy gave me a stiff drink from a pint bottle while his cohorts were still working me over. I developed enough circulation and took off. By the time I delivered that plane and counted my money, I'd probably used most of it.

Neil Cargile ended up becoming president of American Mining and Machinery, a dredging company that specialized in recovering gold and diamonds, and kept flying as a hobby, surviving many close calls. While trying to find him for a visit, I discovered he had also become famous for another hobby: cross dressing. Although not gay, he found joy in wearing women's clothing out and about starting in the 1970s, and his mini-skirted figure was a regular at society events in Nashville and Palm Beach, Florida. The New Yorker magazine even profiled his escapades several months before his August 1995 death from malaria, contracted during a visit to South America. I hadn't heard a thing about him for fifty years, but I wasn't surprised that he kept marching to the beat of his own drummer.

—Reflections—

Looking northwest at downtown Wichita, Kansas, in 1962 - an area where I could find no lodging when I first arrived in the city a decade earlier to work for Boeing.

Chapter 17
Transplanted in Wichita

Following crop dusting during the summer of 1951 and a short stint back with the McKissacks doing sales, I was again in search of income. On a January day of the next year I left the Top Hat Club and happened to walk past an employment office where there was a sign advertising jobs with the Boeing Airplane Company. I was trying to decide whether to go back to Capitol Airways, but I decided to stop in and see what the sign was about. Actually, I would have just passed by the employment office if the word "aircraft" hadn't been involved.

Following an interview with the Boeing representative, I was offered a job in Wichita, Kansas. The man acted very excited about my history. "If that's what you're talking about paying me, I'm not about to go to Kansas," I told him.

"Well, with all the experience you've got, they might place you in a higher pay grade," he said. "If we could get you that, would you come? I'm going to recommend you for it."

In a few days a letter arrived telling me to go to Wichita, where Boeing had established a large manufacturing plant during World War II. I spoke with my friend George Jones about the situation and he said that if I was going he was going, too. George interviewed for a job, was offered the pay level that I had turned down, and accepted. Within a few days, George, his wife and I packed and headed west.

The 750-mile trip from Nashville to Wichita took most of a day. For the last stretch of driving before reaching our destination we headed south on the old State Highway 81 out of Newton, Kansas. Naturally, we were not familiar with the territory, and didn't know that tiny Newton was about 20 miles from Wichita, and that Wichita would be the next place up the road. Some distance out of Newton, at about 11 o'clock on that March night, we drove up a hill and the halo of lights emanating from the largest city in the state jumped out and grabbed us.

We were quite excited about the fact that we were about to be able to get out of the car and stretch our legs. Suddenly, we began to see the outskirts and motel signs. I don't think we stopped at the first one, but as we drove along more into what we considered part of Wichita, we started pulling into motels looking for a place to stay for a night's rest before scoping out the city proper.

It soon looked as if we might have to leave before we even spent one night in town. The worst thing we anticipated was that we would have to put up in cheap motel for a week or so. We thought there wouldn't be a problem finding a temporary place. Stopping at half a dozen motels before giving up, we discovered a pattern: Lighted vacant signs were on until we entered the motel offices and then the clerks said, "Well, we forgot to turn it off." Our final thought was that maybe that was a practice of motels late at night, turning away late-night stragglers. We continued into the downtown area for a real hotel, though we knew it might be more expensive, but at least for one or two nights it would work until we found our way around. Two hotels gave us the same "no room" greeting.

It became evident that the city of 170,000 people had no visitor accommodations. We were essentially stranded in downtown Wichita.

George drove around for a few minutes, not to look for a hotel, but to become more familiar with what the city looked like. We entered from the north on Broadway (Old 81), turned west at some point in South Wichita and eventually found ourselves on Main Street (then a two-way avenue, later changed to one way). We decided that Main ought to give us a bearing of the layout of the town. Main streets usually tell something about that, but not in Wichita. We had no clue Wichita's main drag was actually Douglas Avenue (where all the department stores were), much less that it ran perpendicular to Main. For no special reason we headed north on Main, and, being familiar with what one usually would find in the black area of most major cities, we started to see businesses and signs that indicated we might be where most of the black people probably were, and we also saw an occasional black person getting into a car or walking.

The time was nearing 1 a.m. Of course, all businesses were closed for the night. We drove through the area and thought that, come day, here was where we could find some people to help us. We didn't want to get too far from there so we wouldn't have a problem finding our way back. Near Ninth or Tenth Street, we turned west and immediately found a railroad track. Our first comment was, no wonder we were finding black people; when you find the railroad tracks, that's usually where black people were allowed to establish themselves.

Deciding to park and wait for morning, we found a lighted place just off the railroad track, near some industrial buildings. The radio played while we readied ourselves to sleep, not paying much attention until the announcers started discussing the possibility of tornadoes. Well, we had never been in Kansas, and we didn't pay any attention to the word "possibility." Thus, we grew quite nervous about the weather situation. A little later, we heard there had been an earthquake, but didn't hear where. George, his wife and I looked at each other, "Man, what is this out here? Tornadoes and earthquakes the night we arrive in Wichita?"

About 3 a.m. we fell asleep, and remained undisturbed by tornadoes and earthquakes until the sun woke us about four hours later. We started looking for somewhere to eat and communicate with some locals about a place to stay. Heading back to Main Street and what looked like black businesses, we pulled up in front of a little restaurant that was open for breakfast. While we were having our first meal in Wichita, there were a few other people having coffee and eating. They looked like they hadn't had a nap. At least we had.

George addressed them, "We just arrived in Wichita last night, and we're going to move here to work for Boeing and are looking for a place to stay. We were wondering if any of you had any idea about where we might look, what area of town, or if you might point us in the direction of some housing potential."

"Man, you in trouble," said one of the coffee-drinking guys who didn't look like he'd had any sleep.

Here we were, new to Wichita, and the first words we were hearing was that we were in trouble. We thought we were in trouble the night before, but here in the daytime is a man telling us we're in trouble.

"They have so many folks coming into town to work at Boeing, they ain't got anyplace to stay. Man, there are folks here that work out there that sleep in the same beds in the daytime as the guys that work at night," the coffee drinker said. "But I tell you one thing about this town, if there is any hope for you here, there ain't but two black folks you're going to have to talk to. You got to find Perk Nicholson or Gertrude Johnson. If one of them can't help you, then there's no hope for you here.

"Gertrude has them houses over there, you know where that is. Now, Perk might be down by the pool hall. Ms. Johnson's down on the other side of town in that house where that little liquor store is."

"No, man, we just got here. We don't know anything," George said.

"Now, you know Ninth Street, I'm talking about Ninth Street over on the east side –"

"No, sir, we don't know anything!"

"If you go down the street here, you know, down to the pool hall, go down there and ask for Perk."

Finishing our coffee, George and I looked at each other and understood that we weren't in the right conversation with the right people. We cut the discussion short, but we did know two people's names. We decided to walk and find the pool hall, figuring we could identify a pool hall, though we might not identify Perk Nicholson. On walking in a place that fit our specifications we found somebody who looked a little more intelligent, or not quite as sleepy, and told him we were looking for Perk Nicholson.

"He's not around. What do you want?"

"Well, we were told he might be a good person to direct us to someone who could find us a place to stay – we just got into town. The other person they told us to find was Gertrude Johnson."

"She might be somebody who could help you."

"Where do we find her?"

"She lives on Tenth Street, on the corner of Mosley. You'll know the house, it's got a liquor store that sits almost in the street and it's a big two-story house."

The man gave us directions we could figure out – Main to Murdock, Murdock to Mosley and turn left on Mosley, go down to Tenth Street. We were glad to finally have someone give us instructions that would lead us somewhere.

Even as early-rising and active as we later found Gertrude Johnson to be, she was at home when we found her place. George and I, leaving his wife in the car, knocked on the door, and, on answering, Ms. Johnson immediately came across as a nice-looking, intelligent lady – but very straight-forward; not about to open the door for some strangers to walk in the house. While standing on the porch, we started a conversation with her, beginning with that we were told she might be able to help us out. We mentioned we were in town to work at Boeing and she, being a very political and very informed person, started complaining about how the city and Boeing were handling Wichita's post-war expansion: They knew about the growth and the need for people to work in town, and they should have been doing things about housing, she said.

Only later did I find out she was one of the leading political figures in the city, even though she was black and a Democrat.

Though the conversation took place in Gertrude Johnson's doorway, she began to get more and more open with George and me, expressing concern about the fact that we were here and asking where we came from. Eventually, we earned her confidence and she invited us to bring George's wife out of the car and into the house.

Gertrude hadn't provided any leads yet on where we could live, but at least she was very lucid in discussing Wichita. She said she wasn't surprised that we hadn't found a hotel room and proceeded to explain to us that she owned, at that time, one of the few hotels that took care of black people who came to town – but it was full.

"What were you doing before you decided to come out here and work for Boeing?" Ms. Johnson asked us.

"Well, frankly, I was looking for a job," I said, taking the lead. "I had been flying a crop duster, but the season ended and I was looking for a job and found the Boeing sign."

"Flying an airplane?"

"Yes, I'm a professional pilot. That's my real occupation."

"My goodness, you're only the second colored person I ever saw or heard of flying an airplane," Ms. Johnson said. "They got this guy out here at this plant, and everyone is going wild over this black guy. They talk about what a pilot he is. He's been here for a month or two."

"Who is he?"

"Well, I don't know, but the colored folks around here call him Death."

"What?"

"There's something else they call him, but they always call him Something Death."

"I think I know who's in Wichita. Whitehead has landed in Wichita. I might have to leave town but I am going to spend one night because I'm going to find John Whitehead and we're going to have some fun – because if he's here, he knows where they're having it," I said.

"You know him? You all must be somebody! That man, he is taking over this town, and you know him?"

"I can draw you a picture of what he looks like – he's about that big around, about that tall, and he's sort of got big eyes that sit back in his head. We all used to call him Walking Death. From then on, after he became a military pilot, he was Lieutenant Death, and now, last I heard, he's a captain and I imagine they're calling him Captain Death."

"That's it! That's what they're calling him!"

We talked some more and Ms. Johnson said, "I don't know what I'm going to do, but you all are people who need to be taken care of. All my rental property is either full or I'm trying to remodel and get it ready for rental. It's just going to take some time. What am I going to do with you boys?"

She thought for a minute. "You know, I have a room at the back of the house, where my pop lived. He's down in Oklahoma right now. I could put one of you back there. Let me show you."

We walked back in her house to a small room. "It won't be long before I have something I can put you in, but that's all I got right now," Ms. Johnson said. "I got to get out of here now and get over to get somebody to help me clean up one of these places so I can help you folks."

George spoke up, "I tell you what, if you would let Rip and I us share this room, I'd take my wife back home until you can get something for all of us."

"If you want to," Ms. Johnson said.

"That's all right with me," George said.

I retrieved my things from the car and brought them into the room, and a few minutes later George left for Nashville with his wife. I phoned Augusta and told her what the situation was, but she wasn't expecting to come out for a while anyway because she was teaching and had to wait for the school year to end.

And that concluded my first day in Wichita.

The first house I owned, at 1660 Pennsylvania in Wichita, Kansas, 1953. The two-bedroom residence was also the first permanent home I ever had.

Chapter 18
Gertrude Johnson

Meeting Gertrude Johnson opened a relationship that came as close to friendship as one can expect, though we didn't know that at the time. In later years, I helped Gertrude to the nursing home, sat beside her in the hospital and escorted her body to the cemetery. We became just that close. She came to speak of George and me as if we were her own children.

Gertrude was sizable though not fat, with a muscular build similar to Aunt Lula and my sister Christine, though Gertrude was taller. Like Aunt Lula and Christine, she attended church regularly and at one time earned money doing menial work such as housekeeping and laundry. Wichita had been Gertrude's home since the 1930s, when she moved there with two young daughters; I never knew her marital status. Gertrude saved all the money she could, then started buying run-down properties she would fix up and then rent out or sell at a profit. She also donated money on a regular basis to the Democratic party, very little during her early years in town but more as her income grew. By 1952, when I met her, Gertrude was much respected in Wichita as the owner of a number of businesses and as a political activist. In her later years, she looked forward to attending the state and national Democratic conventions. Gertrude's daughters both graduated from college. One still lived in the house with Gertrude when George and I moved in temporarily, and the other was at Kansas State University working on a master's degree.

With George still gone to Nashville, I was without transportation. Gertrude was in the middle of shutting down a black taxi company she attempted to finance, and happened to have a few cabs that had already been taken out of service. She took me down to a little garage on Mosley Street and told her workers there to set me up with one. With a few days before needing to report to Boeing, I started finding my way around town and repaying Gertrude's kindness by going to her properties and helping repair or fix them up. I'd also go with her to pick up hardware or items in storage.

She knew everybody anywhere she did business, and she introduced me around. For her bail-bond business, we'd get folks out of jail and she'd introduce me to the sheriff and attorneys, "Now here's my boy down here. You ought to know him, he's going to be in this town. No one's going to bother you, Rip. This is attorney so and so; these boys just got out of law school and I'm training them." They'd laugh, "Yes, Ms. Johnson!"

Gertrude was probably in her upper fifties when I met her, and would become an active figure in the local Civil Rights struggle. You mention her to any of the older active political people in the city of Wichita, they say, "Gertrude Johnson? Yeah, we know her." That's how much pull she had. Many of my long-running acquaintances with attorneys, legislators, judges and others started through her.

"I've got to take you to some of my meetings," she'd tell me. Gertrude belonged to Democratic clubs and similar organizations. My association with her did a lot to establish me in my new city.

By the time George returned, Ms. Johnson and I had become so well acquainted that we were just having a good time, and I was almost part of her family. George fell right in, too, because he and I were such good friends and so similar in personality. He and I had stayed in Gertrude's back room for a few days when she said, "You know, I have all these houses. Some of them are full, some of them need work. We need to get something ready for you."

We looked at one small two-story house on the southwest corner of Tenth Street and Wabash. "Fix it up and one of you can have the upstairs and one can have the downstairs. It's yours," Gertrude said. After working, we'd go back to the Johnson residence and she'd say, "If you're workin' for us, we eat together. Come on in the kitchen."

While we were finishing the house, we spent a lot of time riding around Wichita with Ms. Johnson looking at her investments, and one day we ended up by her hotel at Water Street and Pine. She was upset about whoever had been operating the restaurant next door not paying rent and then leaving town with the place messed up. The restaurant served the area and had loyal customers and she also considered it an important asset in supporting the hotel. George and I surveyed the wreckage inside the diner while Gertrude groaned. It hadn't been that long since she had fixed it up for business and now the tenant had gone and messed it up and ...

George said, "Ms. Johnson, why don't you rent this place to me and Rip and we'll fix it and run it?"

"If y'all want this place, here is the key!" she said.

We, or at least I, had given no thought to a restaurant and here she had given George the key. "George, did you say we?"

Well, we were going to have to do it, and we spent the next few days picking the place up. By this time, we'd already pretty much finished the house, staying in the lower level while working on the upper level, and were already working nights at Boeing. While fixing the restaurant, I reviewed our situation and asked, "George, how are we going to run this crap, man?" The more we worked on it, the more we remembered our wives were wanting to move to Kansas, so I said, "Let's let them run it. I don't want to think about hiring somebody to work in here and us not knowing what's going on."

Working our hearts out to get the restaurant finished, we hadn't any time to work on our house's upstairs and had to double our efforts to get it ready before the wives showed up. We put the house into livable condition. George took the upper level and I took the lower level. His wife arrived first because Augusta was waiting for the school year to end. Augusta finally came to Wichita in May 1952 and, due to scarcity of jobs for black home economics teachers, started taking classes at the University of Wichita to earn a master's degree.

After finishing cleaning, polishing and supplying the restaurant, Augusta and George's wife also opened the Water Street Café for breakfast in the morning and dinner in the evening. Augusta liked to joke that she spent time as entertainer Ray Charles' cook, which was true; Ray would come through Wichita fairly often performing in colored bars and juke joints on what was called the Chittlin' Circuit, and he would stop at the Water Street Café and eat Augusta's food.

While working at the café Augusta would leave Camille in daycare at a nearby Catholic school. The teachers there thought Camille was developed enough by the age of four that they allowed her to enroll in kindergarten, which resulted in her being a year ahead in school for the rest of her education. During Camille's first school year Augusta obtained her master's degree, and we sold the restaurant so she could take a teaching job as a long-term substitute in a kindergarten class at a nearby elementary. Though her previous experience had been as a home economics instructor, her love of children helped her transition into the new role. The following school year Augusta was hired on as a full-time kindergarten teacher, and brought Camille to the school for first grade. Augusta eventually became involved in establishing the local Head Start education program for underprivileged children.

When we had time as a family to spend together, we would picnic or travel to Tennessee to visit both Augusta's family and mine. One drive east provided Camille with an education in the racism her mother and I had endured our whole lives. En route through Missouri or Arkansas, Camille said she was hungry, but I kept driving, waiting until I saw a diner that indicated it would serve blacks. Camille couldn't understand why I wasn't stopping, and I didn't want to explain it. Finally, I stopped at an eatery where someone told me to go around to the back door if I wanted service. Instead, I returned to the car and told my daughter the people inside didn't want to sell me anything, which upset her. Within a few years Camille would fully understand what happened, through being exposed to similar racism in Wichita, where blacks still were not allowed in places such as public golf courses and swimming pools.

After growing up orphaned and fending for myself, I was able to appreciate having a fairly orderly family life now that I had a steady routine. George and I spent nights working at Boeing and days sleeping and replacing windows or putting locks on doors for Ms. Johnson while she was busy with her bonding business and other interests. One day George said, "What I'd really like to do is get on the police force. How long do I have to live here before I can apply?"

Ms. Johnson was able to get him hired, along with a friend of hers who was a janitor in city hall. They were among the early colored policemen in the city, joining a few who had been there for a while as tokens.

George's change in careers soon proved worthwhile. After a time of sharing one of Gertrude Johnson's rental houses, George and I started thinking of finding our own places. My family was likely to expand and George and his wife were restless as well. While out on patrol near the eastern border of Wichita's black area, George found two empty lots side by side and told me to take a look. I ended up picking one lot, and he took the other. We built our houses there and became neighbors.

Buying a house constituted a step up in the world for my family and me. Spending my childhood and young adulthood moving frequently, always renting or briefly staying somewhere, I decided that my Boeing job and normal family life provided enough stability to establish a permanent residence. Our new home was small, a two-bedroom one-bathroom affair, but it was still a home. Much of our furniture came from the first apartment in Nashville that Augusta and I rented. Sold to us by the woman who had vacated the place, the furniture followed us to the Wichita house we rented from Gertrude Johnson, and most of it lasted for years to come.

The houses George Jones and I bought were part of a newly constructed development running along northeast Wichita's Pennsylvania Street, at that point near the east edge of the city's African-American area. The east boundary would expand several times in the ensuing two decades through a real estate practice known during that segregated era as "neighborhood busting," whereby a house or two in a white neighborhood would be sold to black families and often prompt the whites to move to more upscale digs, selling their houses to more black families. When I moved onto Pennsylvania Street, the boundary was Hydraulic Avenue, eventually followed in quarter-mile increments by Grove Avenue and then Hillside Avenue, in the vicinity of the University of Wichita. The area west of Hillside and north of the university was inhabited by professors, doctors, attorneys and the like; of course, no blacks lived there. However, a local lawyer and civil rights activist named Chester I. Lewis, who was also one of my flight students, decided to move in during the early 1960s, purchasing a residence by having a white friend front the deal for him. His purchase was followed by another black attorney, and despite occasional harassment early on (including a burning cross in Chester's yard), they essentially ended the neighborhood busting because the area was nice enough that a number of white people didn't care to leave and the country's racial views were starting to change. Years later, that particular area is now fairly mixed between white and black families.

It was while living in the house on Pennsylvania that my second daughter, Bonita was born in 1955. By the time she was two, it became apparent that our family would need a bigger house. We bought one on Volutsia Street, near the Hillside boundary, from a white family that was looking to upgrade. The house had three bedrooms, a den, dining room and full basement,

My second permanent residence in Wichita, on Volutsia Street, was bought from a white family that was vacating the neighborhood.

with which Bonita became familiar after accidentally riding a toy tractor down the stairs. When Bonita was grown, she would comment that she didn't see how we'd been able to fit into the house on Pennsylvania Street.

When I bought the new house, I started renting out the old one on Pennsylvania and purchased another rental house in the area. I don't recall how I learned the principle behind such investing, but it could have been gleaned from Gertrude Johnson: Wealth is created by ownership, and property provides the most permanent form of ownership. With such investing I felt I could contribute to elevating my family to a lifestyle of comfort that I had never known.

Chapter 19
The Boeing Way

The first day I reported to work at Boeing, after being checked out and given identification papers, I was assigned to a shop job in the aircraft final assembly area. My immediate supervisor already had one black in his shop, and at that time there were very few black people in final assembly, so I was placed to work alongside him so he could show me what to do, and because assembly often took two people working together to complete tasks.

Enoch Harper hated my guts for a time while working alongside me as a mechanic at Boeing in the 1950s because he found out I made more money. I won him over and he later worked as a mechanic and pilot with my own aviation business.

Enoch Harper, a young Oklahoman who served as an aircraft mechanic during World War II, started at Boeing a month or so before I got there. He was mechanically oriented and very smart. After working together for some weeks, we were getting along just fine. That came to an end shortly thereafter.

Periodically, maybe every ninety days, we received grade sheets; employees who were doing all right on their grade sheets might be moved up to the next pay grade. One day Enoch and I were talking about the sheets and upgrading, and I said I thought I was supposed to have been higher than a B, as per the agreement I had made with the Boeing representative who came to Tennessee. "You can't start there," Enoch said. "It's got to be a long time before you can get that."

I thought I just didn't understand the coding on my paycheck and didn't pay attention to the subject for a while. Then the conversation came up again with Enoch. When I received the next paycheck, I showed him.

"You're a B?" he yelled, taking off to see the supervisor. "I been here longer and I got no B!"

Enoch came back, took all his stuff out of the tool box, threw it on the shop floor and said, "Show me what you want me to do! You got the B, you know everything. You go do it!" He raised cain to the supervisor about my being hired at that level. For a long time, he was mad, and wouldn't have anything to do with me.

In the meantime, by November 1952 I had started making the rounds to Wichita's small airports, trying to find out more about general aviation in the area and to see who might give me the opportunity to do some part-time flying.

Up to this point I had found only one person who accepted me, at Riverside Airport, now a housing development in North Wichita, near Thirty-seventh Street and Meridian. I had been very coolly addressed at the other little airports I stopped by, but I visited Riverside and its owner, Orville Sanders, didn't have an instructor's license himself but was a licensed mechanic and owned several planes he rented on a part-time basis to instructor pilots to give lessons. Students would come around and he'd find instructors for them. Orville, who became a close friend, told me he'd be glad to have me around and would find some students for me, too, students who had no problem with me being black.

Not long after I started operating at Riverside Airport, Thanksgiving approached and that meant homecoming at Tennessee State University, with a parade and a football game against Kentucky State. Augusta and I had planned to fly home with Camille for the weekend, borrowing Orville's Airmaster, an early four-seat Cessna. The morning before the holiday, snow started to fall. I wanted to take off that afternoon, but the weather didn't clear up and the snow continued to accumulate, falling through the weekend. I witnessed my first Kansas snowstorm on my first Thanksgiving in Wichita, and it resulted in the deepest snow I have ever seen in the area.

I made another valuable aviation-related contact at work one day, when visiting with a foreman named Charlie Byers from the shop next to mine. He owned an airplane and I'd run into him at Riverside Airport, and, in talking, I mentioned I was a flight instructor. That made him comfortable enough to introduce himself. We had a nice conversation, and then the next day or so, the shop superintendent asked my supervisor when I was working and where I was.

"I understand you're a pilot. How long you been that, and where'd you come from?" he asked. "We supervisors have an airplane and we're starting a club out at Rawdon Field. You have a lot of flight hours? How about you come out sometime?"

I knew where Rawdon Airport was because I'd been out there. The Rawdon brothers, who owned the field, concentrated on building a plane called the Rawdon T-1. Herb Rawdon had been the senior partner and former chief designer for TravelAir, a legendary 1920s Wichita-based airline that was absorbed by TWA. He and Gene, his younger brother, had attempted to get the T-1, a plane of their design, accepted by the government for use as a military training aircraft during World War II, which meant the Rawdons would have made a lot of money from mass producing that plane. But they couldn't get their prototype considered and therefore didn't mass produce it as a trainer, although several local manufacturers like Fairchild and Stearman did secure military contracts for building trainers. But the Rawdons made a few, and prior to arriving in Wichita I had seen a picture of a T-1 in a flying magazine and had been very impressed because it looked slick and fun to fly. I didn't remember that the plane was built in Wichita, but when I got to the airport and saw that airplane sitting in front of a building with a sign out front that said "Rawdon Bros.," I said, "That's it!"

Gene Rawdon, an engineer, was hanging around that first time I visited the field, and I said how impressed I was with his plane. That led to my being allowed to ride along when the Rawdons had a pilot doing a test flight.

When I went to Rawdon Field to meet with the Boeing flight club, I found that some of the guys in it were just learning to fly, and some had learned and had flight time. We got along well, and they agreed they wanted me to provide them with instruction. Soon after, they moved the club plane to another airport, Wilson Field, which, after a number of renamings, is now Jabara Airport. The person who ran the fixed-base operation there, Ed Isaacs, was not pleased with their having me come there to give instruction. A compromise was reached with the flying club that I could come there so long as I flew and then left without hanging around the main building, where business was conducted. I just stayed outside, filled out the pilot's logbook, signed it off and left. That was the Wilson Field way of doing business and I accepted it, but I also started instructing another group based at Wilson at that group's request, and that probably didn't sit well with the management either, but the caretaker never barred me from the field.

At Boeing, I was still a peon - but was starting to gain notoriety for my flight experience and because I was instructing supervisors. Such attention started to lead my disgruntled work partner, Enoch Harper, to think I might actually deserve a salary larger than his. His animosity toward me started to ease up, and I convinced him to visit Riverside Airport with me for a flight. "You know, I don't care about flying airplanes, but I'd like to have my aircraft mechanic rating," Enoch said. Flight mechanics need to be certified by the Federal Aviation Administration to sign off on work they do on civilian aircraft. Orville offered to let Enoch help him do some maintenance work, and Enoch eventually decided he wanted to figure out how to make an airplane go up and down, though he still claimed he didn't want to be a pilot.

"If Rip will fly with you, and you want to go up for a lesson, just go up. You don't need to pay to use the plane," Orville told him, and it didn't take Enoch very long to gain enough experience to fly solo.

Regaining a friendly working relationship with Enoch made my job in final assembly more pleasant, but after a year I reached a point where I thought that if that position was the best Boeing was going to offer me, then I wouldn't be hanging out there much longer. I applied to move into the functional test quality area, where, after aircraft parts are assembled, they are tested to make sure they function properly before the plane moves into pre-flight testing on the flight line.

There were no blacks working in that sector, and the personnel department demonstrated it didn't have any interest in placing them there. I would stop by the basement office occupied by personnel, ask about my application's status and be repeatedly told, "We put your name on the list." Men not as qualified as I were being hired to fill the position I applied for. Three inspectors in the quality area who had become friendly with me – Burt Thome, Bob Renner and Walt Headings - saw that I was having a problem with my transfer from final assembly. They started spending time with me visiting about their various duties and about my job qualifications. Of course, our discussions also moved into sports territory, and come spring 1954 somebody suggested I fly the four of us to St. Louis for a baseball game. We discussed the possibility for several days, found a game date and, with a shop guy replacing Walt, flew to St. Louis on a Saturday morning, spent the night and had a good old time. Shortly after returning, Burt told me that Johnny Pierce, the superintendent over quality, wanted to talk to me after work.

Renner and Thome had told Pierce that I was on the list to be moved into quality, and lesser-qualified people were getting hired instead. My meeting with Pierce happened just as I had decided to leave Boeing to try to fly full time. "I hear you want to be in quality," Pierce said when I entered his office. "From what I hear you are very well qualified, and I have no problem with getting you into quality; we can find some place for you. But one of the things that I would have concerns about is if you would do the job just as you saw it and not be influenced by some shop person to accept something you didn't feel was right – whether you would let somebody influence you because you are black and they are white."

"No, I wouldn't do that," I said.

"I'm going to get you transferred into quality, and that 's what I want you to do: Call it like you see it. If you are ever pressured, I want you to let me know and I'll be there. With some of the guys there in the shop, I wouldn't be surprised if they tried to use racism to get their way. In that case I'll be supporting you. You report to personnel and take your transfer over to the supervisor on the floor to put you on the same team with Thome and Renner. They'll take you under their wing till you get started."

I made the trek to the basement personnel office, and said I was moving out of the shop. "Yes, sir, we're working on it, just as soon as we find a spot for you in quality," the clerk said. "No," I said, "I've already been placed in quality and I'm just coming down to get my transfer papers taken care of."

The clerk rummaged through some files. "Oh, the superintendent has already sent your request down here. You're going over to functional test quality." That is where I stayed until Boeing completed its B-47 aircraft program, and then I moved to the flight line. Starting in quality, I was challenged by some of the white shop foremen as to whether my decisions were right, as Johnny Pierce said I would be.

"This control wheel is supposed to move the flap ten degrees from this position, not eleven degrees," I might say. "That's only a one degree difference; that's good enough," a foreman might reply. "How about you call me when it's done right," I'd say and walk off. It took a short time before the challenges ended, which led me to figure that some of the foremen challenged me because I was new rather than black. I never did have to call on the super-intendent to back me up because the foremen gave in and carried on with business as they would with any other person in quality.

My advancement probably owed a lot to the trip to St. Louis with the quality group. It was an example of my expertise and unique hobby turning a situation to my advantage, but it also exemplified the fact that a black wasn't thought good enough unless a white opens the door. Later, I tried to raise the bar again to move to the flight line and was told I should be happy where I was.

—*Reflections*—

The Wichita chapter of the Civil Air Patrol plans a practice search-and-rescue mission at Hamilton Field, south of the city.

Chapter 20
Gaining Respect

During the seven years and some months that I was at Boeing I was involved in a number of community programs such as the National Aviation Youth Program and the Civil Air Patrol. One program included visiting schools to discuss with students the possibilities of aviation as a whole and the possibilities of African-Americans in the field. It wasn't unusual for me to be called on a career day to be part of a panel to talk about flying. In doing this, I usually found myself being the only person of color, particularly the only one qualified as a professional pilot. I was fortunate enough that the people who asked me to participate in those programs gave me reasonable respect because not only was I, in most cases, one of a small number of pilots, but also the highest-qualified pilot in the group. Some were private pilots and some had commercial tickets, but I had all of that, including instrument and instructor certification. It wasn't unreasonable that flying organizations would accept me into their programs and feel that I was qualified to bring a message and serve as a role model to the youth.

Being in the Civil Air Patrol allowed me to speak to many classes on career days. In the 1950s many students had never seen a black pilot before.

When I would be introduced to a class, the students would admire my credentials and accomplishments. For those young people, many of whom were meeting a pilot for the first time and possibly all of whom were meeting a black pilot for the first time, I appeared to be an individual whose future was limited only by the level of the sky. Were the students able to observe me away from my hobby, in the environment in which I had to make a living, they might have been surprised to learn that I could never advance beyond what white supervisors dictated. My recreation allowed me to touch clouds and garner respect, my work forced me back to the ground where I was skipped over for promotions and pay raises. This pissed me off.

Barriers would occasionally come close to limiting my aviation activities, but I often succeeded in spite of them. When I arrived in Kansas, I sought to join the state's Civil Air Patrol, which had been formed during World War II to patrol the nation's borders and perform ground search and rescue flights, and, after the war, continued the search and rescue missions as well as emergency medical runs. In Tennessee I had been allowed to become an officer in the CAP because the state had an all-black squadron. The Kansas CAP officers, who were all white, discussed whether I could transfer my officer ranking into their unit, and decided I could, also accepting the membership of my friend George Jones. Upon joining, I became the only commercial pilot and flight instructor in the local patrol unit. Though I never flew any search missions during my decades in the patrol, I helped establish a headquarters for the CAP's flight activities, the small Hamilton Field, a grass-runway airport outside the Wichita suburb of Derby that is still operating after more than fifty years.

Offsetting the opportunity to promote aviation among young people, membership in the Civil Air Patrol presented me with several racial confrontations. During my time with the Nashville CAP unit, I was sent to the West Texas town of Wink to retrieve a military surplus plane that had been given to us. I rode a bus there and was picked up by the man who was preparing the plane for my flight home. Surprised at my being black, he explained the racial situation in town: It would be a good idea for us to ready the plane and get me out of town that afternoon because I wouldn't be able to find a place to stay for the night. If the plane couldn't be made ready, he said I could stay in his basement and he'd make sure nobody would bother me. As appealing as that offer sounded, I decided to take my chances with flying elsewhere for overnight lodging. Taking the plane for one test pass around the man's field, I headed to a place in Arkansas that

I knew was friendly. I have never returned to Wink, Texas.

In Kansas, I flew with the Wichita branch of the CAP on a routine morning multi-plane flight about 130 miles to Junction City, Kansas, with each pilot carrying along a CAP cadet. We were to have lunch and fly back to Wichita. We arrived in Junction City and went where someone said we could find a good lunch on the main drag, only to walk in the place and be told that George Jones and I - the only blacks in the group - would have to leave, though everyone else could remain. The whole group walked out. To keep from further embarrassment, a three-member survey team fanned out to find a place where we could all dine.

At this time in Kansas, some social changes were occurring, most notably the U.S. Supreme Court case of Brown v. the Topeka Board of Education, a big move toward integration, though it would take decades to be fully implemented. When people often ask me what things were like in the South, I want to reveal to them that racism was not unique to the lower half of the country. My first night in Wichita looking for a motel, not being able to be seated with my comrades in Junction City and, later, being ordered out of a restaurant in McPherson by a manager with a meat cleaver serve to illustrate this. Many people may be surprised such incidents happened in Kansas. African-Americans from small communities with practically no other African-Americans were generally accepted by the other towns-people; they don't realize that this was not the case for those blacks who gathered in major cities.

As I mentioned, flying opened doors for me that wouldn't otherwise have been. If flying didn't open the doors, it certainly led me to them. When the Boeing Flying Club moved to the just-opened Wichita Municipal Airport, later Mid-Continent Airport, I renewed an acquaintance with Jack Dixon, a Boeing inspector who had taken charge of the flight program for the fixed-base operation at the new airport, which included a Beech dealership, and allowed me to do some instructing there. One friend I encountered was a medical doctor just out of school who was new in town and wanted to fly, "Tex" Butler. We knew each other from Nashville, where he spent weekends playing saxophone in a band of his medical school classmates. He became my first African-American flight student in Wichita, and also my first black student there to purchase an airplane, perhaps the first person of color in the city to own a plane. He was the first black in Wichita to own a Corvette as well. I brokered the deal between him and Dixon's Beechcraft dealership for the new Bonanza, and that constituted my first involvement with an aircraft sale in Wichita. A year after getting his pilot rating, "Tex" relocated to Amarillo, Texas, to be near family.

Dr. Tex Butler moved to Wichita, Kansas, and was my first black flight student in the city to buy a plane, possibly the first African-American in Wichita to do so. He was also among the first in town to own a Corvette.

While at the municipal airport, I would notice a well-dressed older man hanging around, taking lessons or visiting people. What I did not know was that he was Marcellus Murdock, the publisher of The Wichita Eagle, one of the most influential publications in the state. Murdock, the son of the paper's founder, thought it odd that a black man would be hanging around the airport, and he started asking around about me. Finding I was as highly rated as a pilot as anyone around there, he told one of his reporters to write a feature about me. This writer put the project off for a while, until Murdock told him one Thursday to have it ready for the Sunday paper.

The writer didn't know how to contact me, but Murdock told him I worked for Boeing. Then Murdock himself called the head of Boeing Wichita, J. Earl Schaefer. I was on the flight line when a guy motored up on a scooter from the main office, saying I was wanted there right away. My supervisor was very concerned about what was going to happen to me because he wasn't given any instruction other than to release me to go. I hopped on the scooter and was shown into a private room where this reporter told me the story about Murdock and the Sunday paper. The resulting article, complete with a picture of me, brought me a lot of phone calls from people who knew I was in town and some who were surprised that such a person existed in Wichita – all in all, a very positive response. After that, those who had tread carefully around me became more comfortable visiting, maybe because they had never had an article written about them.

My photo as it appeared in a 1955 Wichita Eagle feature story, during the time I worked at Boeing and flew when I could. The exposure resulted in more respect being given to me at work and in the community.

One call I received, partly through my exposure in The Wichita Eagle, was from a young attorney named Stan Wisdom. He had done some legal work to form a flying club for a small group of employees of the Southwestern Bell telephone company. Though the club members didn't have any money to pay him, they offered to let him use the plane to learn to fly if he found an instructor. Stan had a desire to learn, and so accepted the proposition in lieu of pay. One club member told him about me being an instructor.

We arranged to meet at Rawdon Airport on what turned out to be a nice day for flying. Stan easily identified me, having seen my picture in the paper and noticing I was the only black around. After exchanging greetings, we sort of looked each other up and down and I noticed he happened to be wearing a pair of white and tan shoes exactly like the pair I had on – a good sign. We walked over to his club's plane, a fabric-body, 65 horsepower Taylorcraft BC-12 that could reach about 80 mph if the nose was down. I gave Stan an introduction, "This is an airplane." And he says to this day, "Right away, I decided this guy was going to teach me everything; he didn't even think I knew this was an airplane."

Stan and I worked through the program, and he proved to be a very good student and very sharp; the main thing I respected about him was that he accepted instruction well. He was an attorney and not a flight instructor, which is not a bit of knowledge carried by all flight students. Shortly before I gave him his final check for his license, he asked, "Why are you not into flying full time?"

"No one will give me a full-time job."

"Well, why don't you start your own business?" he said.

"Well, I have an answer for that too. I don't have the money."

"You know, if sometime you'd like to start your own business, I know people who make investments in things and help form businesses, and if you get the idea you'd like to do something like that, come talk with me."

I didn't think about the suggestion much at the time, but it was a statement that returned to my mind a couple of years later.

Chapter 21
Flying Club

I formed my own flying club in the mid-1950s consisting of several of my students and people they knew. My main purpose in doing this was so that I could have a plane at my disposal rather than relying on the other clubs or airports I worked for. Most of the people in the club shared a similar situation, having learned to fly, they lacked the money to purchase their own aircraft. Each person paid a percentage of the plane's price, and thereafter operating and maintenance costs for the aircraft. We enjoyed being able to take out a plane when our schedules permitted.

Foremost among the five initial investing members of my club was attorney Chester I. Lewis, my first black flight student who obtained a license. The other people he and I brought on all happened to be white. The lone female, Virginia Snyder, a partner in the Bunny Car Wash on Wichita's George Washington Boulevard, was one of my students. Club membership changed from time to time and at one point included a young plastic company owner and law student named Ray Hodge who would often fly to Oklahoma City for training with his classmate Vern Miller, who became one of the most notable Kansas lawmen of the last half century.

Another eventual member was a photographer with an office downtown on Central Avenue. He was just learning to fly, and I flew with him on a couple of occasions to Kansas City, noticing that he always carried along a brown envelope, which he would pass on to somebody in K.C. Prior to him being certified as a pilot, he asked me to make a trip to Kansas City without him, meet someone (no name given) and pass along one of those brown packages. I did not then and have no idea today what was in that package, but a year or so later, after both the photographer and I had left the flying club, he was arrested and convicted of child pornography charges.

We first based the club and our Piper Tri-Pacer at Ken-Mar Airport, one of the names of the former Wilson Field in northeast Wichita, and then soon moved to the municipal airport. The 135 horsepower, all-fabric Tri-Pacer, so named because of its tricycle landing gear, was one of the first planes to have decent ground handling due to its lack of tail wheel. The four-seat plane was rated to fly at slightly more than 100 miles per hour, and served as a good basic aircraft for recreational pilots. Sadly, one of the club's novice members, a medical doctor, died southwest of Wichita while taking the Tri-Pacer on a night flight. Replacing the plane, the club upgraded to a locally manufactured, all-metal, four-seat Cessna 172 (which was more comfortable than the Tri-Pacer) and later a Cessna 182.

In the late 1950s, while giving Chester Lewis some advanced flight training toward his instrument rating, I had him make some instrument approaches at the Hutchinson, Kansas, airport. At one point we were within miles of the airport at nearby McPherson, and I suggested we stop there to have a bite to eat. A regular stop for many other instructors from the Wichita airport, the McPherson airport was situated along a highway, and its service building provided gas to highway traffic on one side and aircraft on the other. A diner a few yards away also served food to both air and highway travelers. Chester landed the plane and we taxied past some aircraft that I recognized as being from Wichita. Walking into the diner, I received greetings from the Wichita pilots who were eating. With all the tables full, Chester and I sat on two of the stools at the diner's counter and proceeded to wait a very long time for service. The waitress passed by us repeatedly during trips from the kitchen to the tables, Chester finally caught her attention and indicated that we would like to be served. "Wait a minute," she said, and then continued to wait on other customers. Then, the cook approached us.

"What do you boys want," the cook asked.

"We want to be served," Chester replied.

"You can't be served here."

"Why?" Chester asked.

"You know why."

"No, I don't know why."

"Get out," the cook said.

"Why?" Chester asked. With that the cook grabbed a meat clever; Chester and I decided to leave, and were followed by the rest of the pilots. Outside and angry, Chester used a payphone on the side of the building to try to call the McPherson city government to complain, but reached no one worth complaining to. Later Chester sent a letter, and received a response inviting him back to town. He returned to the diner without me, ordered and paid for food but then refused to

Wichita attorney and Civil Rights activist Chester I. Lewis and I visit the Tuskegee Institute campus during a Negro Airmen International convention. The statue is of Booker T. Washington, the institute's founder.

eat it. There was no telling how that bigoted cook may have prepared or altered the meal. In the years following, Chester continued to be an active pilot and aircraft owner, and we remained close until he died.

Having access to the club plane ended up being as convenient as I expected it to be. My central concern for traveling was to visit Tennessee as often as I could to see my Aunt Lula and Uncle Fred, who were becoming more frail in their health. My family and I made a tradition of flying to Tennessee for Labor Day and Christmas, and sometimes on other occasions.

Shortly after Fred died, in the mid-1950s, Augusta, Camille and I drove east to bring Aunt Lula to Wichita for a few days. In showing her around town, I took her to see the club plane, by this time a Cessna 182. Camille climbed into the back seat and Aunt Lula followed while I explained how the plane worked and sat in the pilot seat and Augusta sat in the front passenger seat. I hadn't thought about taking the plane up, but Aunt Lula broached the subject, "Well, are you going to fly it?" She had never been flying with me in all the time I had lived in Tennessee.

"Do you want to?" I asked.

"I got in this thing, didn't I?"

It was a lovely, calm evening, the type I enjoyed taking first-time passengers up during, to see the lights of the city. Aunt Lula became involved in looking around and we stayed in the air for about an hour. "What do you think about it?" I asked her.

"There ain't nothing to it," she said.

That was my clue Aunt Lula was ready to fly regularly, the orientation around Wichita being a good seller. At the end of the first visit to Wichita, I flew her back home, and from then on she always flew to visit.

What amazed me later was that on the way back from Tennessee once with her, we flew over an area with some lakes in which storms are known to develop quickly, and we hit one that gave us turbulence so bad it knocked the hat off her head. "How are you getting along?" I asked her.

"All right with me," she said. "You're driving this thing."

That really was impressive. We had gone through turbulence that was rough for me, but she just passed it off.

—*Reflections*—

After leaving Boeing, I established Aero Services, the first African-American-owned aviation operation in the Air Capitol of the World.

Arlene Nelson was Aero Services' office manager for sixteen years. She earned her pilot's license and delivered planes for the business.

Chapter 22
Fixed-Base Operation

It wasn't until sometime in 1958 that I became discouraged with my prospects at Boeing and my prospects in general. Though constantly on the lookout, I still had not been able to find a full-time flying job, even though I knew people who were establishing businesses. No one would offer me a full-time job as part of their organization, though they would allow me to do some part-time flight instruction. I submitted my name to be on the list of candidates for possible hire as Federal Aviation Administration flight inspectors, a job that would have paid much more than Boeing. For some time I annually updated my application, but never received any offers. At that time possibly one black person was employed as an FAA inspector, but maybe none.

At Boeing, I noticed that people hired into and working beside me in the quality area were trained and immediately moved to a level above me. I became concerned enough about it to question my supervisor, and he thought that I should be very pleased that I was one black person who was employed in quality control and could come to work everyday in a collared shirt and starched pants looking clean. Why should I think I should go any further when there were white people there in the crud building airplanes?

In February 1959, my supervisor, Don Harndon, gave me an employee performance review of 77 out of 100 points, the most points possible without reaching "exceptional" status. He wrote, "You have maintained a very high standard ... With renewed effort on your part it should be possible for you to reach the higher level." Although I had seven years under my belt, I was not graded as highly as many of the whites Don reviewed who hadn't been on the job as long as I.

That didn't sit right, but I accepted it as being the way things were and started thinking about other career options. Later came another opportunity for advancement at Boeing, when someone was wanted to do some flight test evaluation work, not as a pilot, but involving some of the equipment in the airplane. I attempted to be transferred into that job and was told that management didn't think I met the requirements. The job was instead filled by a young white person just out of college who had never flown an airplane or had anything to do with that type of operation.

These things kept building up on me and that's what pressured me to act on my desire to leave Boeing and pursue flying full time, as tough as I knew that prospect would be. I remembered the young attorney who told me to give him a call if I ever started thinking about starting my own business. It had been about two years since I had contact with Stan Wisdom, but he remembered his offer and said it was still good. Stan said I should sit down and develop a plan as to how I might start a business and where I'd do it. Stan returned the first business proposal I submitted to him, saying the plans weren't of a large enough scale to attract investors. Not wanting to continue my employment with Boeing, I was determined to devote my energy to building a full-time flying career, and in wanting to be sure of getting financial backing for a business of my own I had simplified my ideas too much. Stan, a successful lawyer who had experience financing business ventures, further discussed with me how to bulk up my proposal and what kind of other preparatory work I needed to do before he tried to attract business partners.

My proposed venture ultimately consisted of setting up an independent fixed-base operation at one of Wichita's small airports, offering maintenance, fueling, flying lessons, chartered flights and, eventually, aircraft sales. Setting my plan into action would be a major step forward for me and for the city of Wichita. If my plan for starting my own business worked, I would be the first African-American to run his own aviation operation in the Air Capital of the World.

I had researched locations and then approached the Rawdon brothers, whose weed-ridden airstrip in what was then rural east Wichita sat mostly unused because they were no longer manufacturing aircraft, limiting their activities to making parts and occasional plane modifications. The grass runway was mowed only once in awhile, when it needed to be used, and the usable part of it was fairly short because of electrical lines at the south end. Aside from the Rawdons' main building, which was several hundred yards from the road, a large metal Quonset hangar sat near the part of the Rawdons' land that bordered Central Avenue, across from the Beechcraft plant and airport. The hangar, situated parallel to Central, had a walk-in door on one side and an ill-fitting hangar door that opened on the field side, where planes could be brought in and out. Essentially, Rawdon Airport didn't have anything to lose from me setting up shop there; both the airfield and I had nowhere to go but up.

Stan Wisdom, after going over my revised plan, which included a leasing agreement for Rawdon Airport, got in touch with five other people he thought would be valuable partners in the incorporation of the new business.

Someone told me it was a good idea to choose a business name that would appear first in the phone book, and I thought of my former teacher Jimmy Taylor's Nashville flight business, Aero Services Inc.

Five of the six investors, including Stan, Cessna aeronautic engineer Dan LaMaster and I, put in an initial $1,800 each (at $100 per share of the business). The sixth and most significant member of Aero Services' board of directors, local cattleman Roy Holloway, invested $3,600 and his Piper Comanche 250. The Comanche had been a Stan-encouraged purchase Roy made, but Roy seldom used it. The other planes in Aero Services' fleet of three included a Taylorcraft BC-12 and a Luscom 8A, whose owner, Hal Snow, was also a board member.

We all agreed that I, as manager and sole employee of Aero Services, would receive a set salary in addition to a certain number of shares per year, which Stan planned would build up over time to make me the majority owner. Additionally, I was given the title of vice president; Holloway, as majority shareholder, served as president for the time being.

It was mid-1959 when the ball really started rolling. With the logistics figured out and Boeing being in one of its layoff periods, I put my name on the voluntary layoff list so I could get a clean break from the company while drawing a regular paycheck a little longer. I was set up for business by October. An eight-foot long wooden table placed at the closed end of the metal hangar served as my office. The telephone company set up a phone connected to a loud bell that I could hear if I was out mowing the runway or doing other chores. Answering machines were still years away, but if my phone rang a certain number of times, the call would be forwarded to an answering service I paid to take messages, a handy arrangement if I happened to be flying with a student or charter customer.

With winter coming, the board of directors agreed I should find someone to construct a building on the south side of the hangar. Dan LaMaster and I drew up a floor plan for some office and storage space. We investors called in favors with some business contacts to get new windows and doors, a concrete floor and a gas heater, in some instances trading stock for services.

Other modifications to the facilities and staff at Rawdon Airport were made over the next several years, a time period in which loans were made to Aero Services thanks to Earl Chandler at Wichita's Union National Bank. Unique as a loan officer, he understood my business and did what he could to help it grow, which was unusual because many banks would not loan money to people of color. Our business relationship turned into a long-lasting friendship.

In the way of Aero Services' facilities, for the first few months of operation, we fueled planes using the Rawdons' gas pump, which was located in tall grass away from the Aero Services building. I negotiated a deal in February 1960 with a pair of brothers who owned several Phillips 66 gas stations in Wichita and supplied gas to several other local stations. George and Don Harpool put in tanks and pumps at Rawdon without requiring any money down; they accepted payment as we pumped fuel into the planes. We agreed they would be Aero Services' exclusive fuel supplier, and it was a good arrangement for the Harpools to get involved on the business's ground floor. As time passed and the Harpools hung around Rawdon Airport, they developed a desire to buy their own plane. Don had been a military pilot, and I gave George lessons. They eventually bought four upgrades through me.

The next issue to be addressed was the fact that people stepping outside our door often stepped into dirt or mud. We found a person in the construction business, L.A. Knebler, to put asphalt around the building and around the gas pumping area. I traded him a used Cessna 182 for his services. Similarly, we needed concrete for the areas where we tied down planes, our three, plus those owned by the growing number of pilots using Rawdon Airport as their base. One of my flight students happened to be associated with a concrete company that was doing a job nearby, and he arranged for trucks hauling leftover concrete to stop at Rawdon and dump where we needed paving. It was a mutual convenience because Aero Services didn't have to spend money on the deal and the concrete company didn't have to look for an out-of-the-way spot to dispose of its leftovers.

The first addition to the staff, Woody Pratt, was brought on after winter 1959 construction was completed. He was a retiree who worked inexpensively servicing planes, and the two of us plus some part-time mechanics held down the fort for more than a year, until I hired my former flight student Larry "Pete" Shepard as my first full-time mechanic. I had given him flying lessons during his senior year of high school, and then he left to become an aircraft mechanic in the military. His return to Wichita several years later in search of work happened just as I was looking for more help. A similar situation brought to me a recently discharged Air Force officer, James Calhoun. Though he had obtained an education degree at the Tuskegee Institute, he entered the military, becoming a maintenance officer. On discharge he decided to take an aircraft mechanic training course, found he liked it and became licensed by the FAA. He called me looking for work. Later he would establish a high school aircraft maintenance training program for the Wichita school system.

The total personnel of Aero Services, my fixed-base operation at Wichita's Rawdon Airfield, January 2, 1961. From left: Bob Colbert, Larry "Pete Shepherd, Woody Pratt, me and Dan Lamaster.

When I started spending quite a bit of time piloting charter flights, I found that we needed more scheduling control and record keeping, so we brought on an office manager, a man who was soon replaced by Arlene Nelson, who would stay with Aero Services until it closed in 1976. Having an office manager to keep track of what was going on allowed us to book more flight training sessions, which in turn led me to hire other instructors to lessen my load, Gene Langston and Paul Knepp, both former military pilots. Sadly, Gene was involved in the most serious accident of Aero Services' existence. While on a training flight, he decided to have his student perform some crosswind takeoffs and landings, which can be tricky. The Rawdon runway ran north and south, the direction the wind was blowing, so Gene had the student go to Ken Mar Airport, a little more than a mile away. While the student was practicing the crosswind exercises, the Taylorcraft spun in and crashed, severely injuring the student, who would recover, and killing Gene.

I worked literally day and night, and business grew steadily. For two years our income came from providing charter flights, flying lessons and selling and trading used aircraft. Then one day in 1962 a man named Don Benedict breezed in flying a four-seat Mooney M-21, looking for someone to try it out and to see if Aero Services was interested in becoming a Mooney dealership.

Don, regional sales manager for the Kerrville, Texas-based Mooney Aircraft, grabbed board member Dan LaMaster. After the test run, Dan said he would need to speak with the manager about the Mooney and that Don should come back when I was around.

The Aero Services board had been discussing becoming a new-plane dealership, so Don Benedict's appearance was opportune. After flying the Mooney, Dan strongly recommended that I try it out.

Benedict returned a few days later to take me up, and the Mooney did, indeed, impress me enough to make me want to sell it through Aero Services. I asked Don what the difference would be between a dealership and distributorship, and he said that dealers often bought one plane at a time from Mooney while distributors had to commit to several planes and be responsible for establishing other dealers in their area. Distributors also made money selling replacement parts.

1 Flight Instructions

COMPLETE FLIGHT SUPPLIES

PRIVATE PILOT
COMMERCIAL
INSTRUMENT
INSTRUCTORS
ART
LOW COST FINANCING
FAA APPROVED SCHOOL
FAA DESIGNATED FLIGHT
EXAMINER ON FIELD

Veterans Program Approved

RATINGS IN
SINGLE ENGINE
MULTI - ENGINE
HELICOPTER

2 Sales

Mooney
Distributor & Dealer

The Plane For Business
or Pleasure

Mooney — The Greatest For
Speed And Comfort

WE CAN HELP YOU WITH YOUR
FINANCING & INSURANCE

3

Shop & Services

A&P MECHANICS ON DUTY HAVE
BEEN FACTORY TRAINED IN AIRFRAME
& ENGINE OVERHAUL.

COMPLETE OVERALL ANNUALS
PARTS — COMPLETE REPLACEMENT
SERVICE
FOR MOONEY
FOR BENDIX
FOR GOODYEAR

LINE SERVICE
OIL PHILLIPS & AERO SHELL
80 AND 100 OCTANE
WASH & WAX AIRPLANES
HANGERS & TIE-DOWN
NIGHT OR MONTHLY

My flight operation offered a variety of services.

When Benedict asked me whether I wanted to take him up on a dealership offer, I surprised him by saying I'd rather be a distributor. The other Mooney distributorships had been in business a long time, had nice-looking facilities and had white owners. Compared with them, Aero Services looked like a questionable risk. On his departure, Don said I'd hear from him soon.

"Soon" turned into weeks, and I called him to see what was going on. He hemmed and hawed and finally said Mooney's vice president, Norm Coffman, would fly to Wichita to see me. Norm flew in and explained the situation, "Don expressed concern to me about you being black, but I've checked you out and everyone in the aviation business here has nothing but good things to say about you. How would you like to be a Mooney distributor? Fly down to Kerrville and visit the factory and see what you think."

This Beech Model 18 was one of Aero Services' fleet.

The opportunity came at the right time, shortly after we had paved Rawdon Airport's grass runway and received Federal Communications Commission clearance for ground-to-air radio transmitting for our planes. Additionally, the Wichita district chief for the Federal Aviation Administration, James Colton, recommended me to be an FAA pilot examiner; over the next three decades I would certify several thousand students as FAA-approved pilots.

During the first week of July 1962, Pete Shepard and I flew to Kerrville, Texas, to tour Mooney's facilities. Everything went along nicely, and then after dinner the director of marketing, who was in charge of taking care of us, handed me keys for a motel room and a station wagon. Pete and I had no desire to spend the rest of the evening in a motel room, so the two of us and, as Pete recalls, a Mooney dealer from India started looking for bars. After the first few denied us service, I mentioned that we better start looking for the railroad tracks, where the colored bars probably would be. The next day, I told the marketing man what happened, and he promised it would be taken care of. I can only guess that Mooney came down hard on the local businesses, because I didn't have much trouble there again. Kerrville was dependent on Mooney Aircraft, and it would make sense that what Mooney wanted, Mooney got. It turned out that I integrated Kerrville, Texas. On future trips there I would return to the businesses that had previously thrown me out, often taking with me my acquaintances from the railroad tracks.

Selling Mooney aircraft in Wichita, the home of the biggest-selling small-airplane companies, Beech and Cessna, would be difficult. Mooney had actually been based in Wichita following World War II, manufacturing 290 Mooney Mites, a single-seat plane with retractable landing gear and a forward-swept "backward" tail.

Mooney airplanes featured "backward" tails.

Founder Al Mooney supposedly moved the operation to Kerrville to be near a family dairy farm, but competition from Beech and Cessna likely also influenced the decision. Despite the company's previous Wichita history, my confidence in my sales ability never wavered, and within a few years Aero Services became one of Mooney's top distributors worldwide, joining the company's million-dollar club. During the time Aero Services worked with Mooney, corporate mismanagement caused two production shutdowns. The final shutdown, in 1970, would cause a major financial disaster for Aero Services. For some time Mooney had an agreement with its dealers that part of their profits would be given to the corporation in exchange for certificates that could be redeemed for the money later with interest. This system allowed Mooney to invest more in research and development, etc., and would have been good for the dealers had the company not bankrupted. Aero Services was left holding $100,000 in worthless certificates. Mooney itself eventually was resurrected years later, and is currently back in business.

An advertisement for an event Aero Services hosted at Rawdon Airfield in 1965. Note the Mooney Aircraft sign on the main building and the Mooney airplane sitting in front.

Mooney dealers Buford Scott (left) and his father Buell talk with me at a 1960s air show (the Blue Angels are in the background). Whenever I visited them in Western Kansas, I was the only black in Stanton County.

—Reflections—

George Johnson (left, with me in 1981 at Beech Airfield) lived near the Water Street Café when my wife operated it in the 1950s, won the Distinguished Flying Cross during the Vietnam War and became the first black in a management position at Beech.

Chapter 23
Sky Tales

In piloting charter flights, giving lessons and taking aircraft to customers around the country, I accumulated thousands of hours of flying time and numerous stories involving customers, close calls and other incidents. Here are a few:

• •

To place in perspective the difference between aviation today and aviation during the first years I flew, it's worth noting the progress in communication and navigation. Pilots today may find it hard to believe what we used decades ago, such as solely aural skills. To help pilots stay on course, transmitters set up at checkpoints along flight routes emitted two radio frequencies, one for each ear, to be heard over a pilot's headphones. This constituted what is known as airways. The hum of the frequencies alerted the pilot whether to steer toward the left or right, and if the plane were on exact course, the frequencies would interlock to form a constant sound. On occasion an aircraft would be on course so exactly that at a certain point when passing directly over the transmitter - an area known as the cone of silence - the sound would stop. For night flying, pilots could keep on route by following rotating light beacons, as long as there was visibility of more than twenty miles.

Early radios consisted of single-crystal sets that could not transmit and receive simultaneously. Pilots had to alert communication stations to provide them time to twist the radio crank to find the frequency that the station was on, before initiating conversation.

Navigation improved with the availability of the automatic direction finder, or ADF, which relieved pilots from cranking. A needle would point in the direction of a low frequency station's immediate location. The system worked well except low frequency transmissions are highly susceptible to thunderstorms and interruption by elements. Eventually, there emerged very high frequency omni-directional range, or VOR, which allowed a 360-degree reading of accurate location to or from communication stations. This coupled with whistle-stop tuning for radios (when cranking the radio, a whistle would alert the pilot with a whistle sound when the receiver was matched to a transmitter, eliminating the need for a long count) made me think aviation had arrived at a level of navigation that would never get better.

Needless to say, with the advances that have taken place, all these old methods are so long forgotten that few people still flying were ever exposed to them. There was a time when technology took years to progress, but it now does so on an exponential basis, every year it seems. If years ago I had the indicators, computers and other gauges now common, I could have avoided a number of frightening situations.

. . . .

One close call caught me while I was returning to Wichita from Memphis after buying a used Piper Tri-Pacer. It was late fall or early winter, and this aircraft had a minimum of navigation and communication equipment and no heated piotot, which enables the airspeed indicator. I was en route to Wichita, about 100 miles out, and I started encountering a light drizzle. The ground at this time was covered with a light snow and the temperature was dropping. A few miles further, I encountered an overcast and decided to descend and proceed into town at a very low altitude, scud running. Entering the Flint Hills area east of Wichita, I encountered conditions where the overcast had descended to the ground and as I attempted to make a turn, I found myself in the overcast.

I attempted to climb to an altitude hoping to top out but couldn't. Suddenly my Piper's fabric wings were covered in ice. I lost airspeed and attitude instruments, and lack of ability to continue to climb. I found myself losing control of the plane and was in a dive and spiral. Momentarily I found myself neglecting my basic instrument flight training. Remembering to look at my primary indicators – my magnetic compass and needle ball – saved me from crashing.

I made a 180-degree turn and descended until I was in clear air, and landed at a small grass strip nearby. Upon contact with the ground there was a loud noise, as a result of all the ice that had been hanging on the plane breaking off and falling away. After landing and listening to low frequency radio, I heard the weather in Wichita consisted of scattered clouds. So I took off and climbed above the weather and flew into Wichita, safely completing a very uncomfortable flight.

. . . .

My most dangerous experience trying to sell a plane resulted in my first and only actual near-death experience. In aircraft sales, the demonstration flight can be dangerous because you allow the customer to have a chance to get the feel of the aircraft controls. On one occasion I allowed myself to extend this opportunity too far.

One of my sales people, Tom Hemphill, asked me to go close a deal with him in Chanute, Kansas, with a flying club of about ten people. Tom had met several times with this group attempting to sell a used Mooney M-20A, 1959 model. Our arrival and meeting went well, with Tom demonstrating the plane to several club members. The final purchase decision was put on hold because an influential group member hadn't shown up. Several phone calls were made, and he finally showed after dark. On his arrival, he left no doubts that he was the person who knew it all, and took over. We guessed what we'd be in for when he made his first comment, "A couple of you guys get in here so I can go fly it." All the other club members had flown the Mooney in the daytime, but he didn't care.

Tom's explanation on loading procedure for the plane was disregarded. The pilot is supposed to get in first, but the jerk directed two club members to get in the plane's backseat. At this time Tom firmly suggested, "Rip why don't you give the demonstration ride?"

As I got in the plane, I explained the handling procedures for the customer, who was going to pilot it but was paying little attention. He started the engine with the Vernier throttle fully opened, but he couldn't figure out how to close it and then did some other things that should have indicated a reason to abort the mission. But my instinct as a salesperson persevered.

I decided there wouldn't be much explanation on this flight. After proceeding to the runway and taking off, I personally retracted the flaps and gear without telling the pilot. He turned out of the air traffic pattern with full power. After climbing a couple thousand feet, he leveled the plane off and saw how fast it would go in regular flight with full throttle. "This airplane really will go," he said.

By this time he had taken the plane into the Flint Hills where there was total darkness, no ground lights to allow us to judge our position. After some turns in level flight, the pilot said he was going to stall the plane. Pulling back rapidly on the control, the attitude of the plane reached vertical by the time it hit stall speed. The stall occurred with the pilot's hand on the throttle in full position. He attempted to pull out of the stall by pushing the control wheel forward, but the plane fell into a spiral at full throttle, and the control wheel locked in place. This happened in pitch dark with no visible horizon. In a moment the plane's airspeed indicator had passed redline speed and peaked out.

The plane was headed toward the ground at top speed, and though I tried to gain control, I couldn't. The pilot panicked, froze on the control and was destined to kill us all. Within seconds, all my life past and present flashed through my mind. Unless you have encountered it, you wouldn't understand how fast thoughts move in such a situation. I was convinced we were going to die. Fear disappeared, and I entered a state of peacefulness.

Suddenly the pilot let go of everything and yelled, "Take it over, Rip!"

Gaining consciousness immediately, I got the plane into level flight, pulling up in a valley. The passengers in back claimed that recovery was made at a height below the trees and hills on either side of the plane. That valley was our salvation, saving us by feet or possibly inches.

There was no communication among any of us until we landed. We exited the aircraft, and the pilot said to the members of the club on the ground, "That's a fast airplane, but I think some of you guys might get into trouble flying it." With that, I said "Thanks, guys; Tom, let's go," indicating to him that he should fly us to Rawdon Airport. He pressed me for information about what happened, because he knew I wouldn't abort a sales pitch without a good reason.

A few days later, the two passengers who had sat in the back of the plane, drove to my office to thank me for saving their lives. "We blame ourselves somewhat," they said. "We saw how you were wrestling with the controls, and we should have landed the biggest blow we could on that guy's head. But we didn't." In the years since, I have spoken with only a few people who have been so close to death that they have reached total peacefulness. It is a feeling that can't be expressed or experienced through words.

I never heard from the pilot.

. . . .

One man who owned a plane but didn't have a license hired me to pilot him for several months in the early 1960s. He was a building contractor who needed to fly around Kansas, Nebraska and Missouri to oversee construction of post office buildings. He had a brain tumor and was taking some very powerful injected medication. If he ran out of medicine, the pain in his head would cause him to become extremely angry without warning. On a trip to Oklahoma, he decided to take some of his construction foremen to lunch and invited me along. "No, I'll just hang out with the plane," I said, knowing what would entail accompanying whites into a diner. "Come on," he insisted. We sat down in the restaurant and waited to be served, and we kept waiting until the contractor grabbed a waitress, who got the manager, who said, "We don't serve coloreds."

"If you discriminate against him, you are discriminating against me," the contractor told the manager. The contractor was showing signs of needing medication, with the vein in his forehead bulging out. "Now, we are going to be served. Understood?"

"Yeah, we're hungry," one of the burly foremen growled.

We were quickly served.

＊ ＊

One of my competitors in Wichita had quite a reputation, and if you ask some old local aviators, they'll each have a Jack Fluornoy story. He had been a Boeing employee, but left to start the flight training operation at Mid-Continent Airport, which included helicopters.

When I visited Fluornoy once in the mid-1960s, he asked me whether I had ever flown a helicopter, which I hadn't. He told his instructor to take me for a demonstration ride in a Bell. I was never so outdone by a flying machine; I couldn't keep one side up or the other side down. Flustered by my entire lack of ability, I immediately signed up for instruction upon landing Several days later I had my first lesson in the Bell, and after a few hours had mostly figured it out. Shortly before my second lesson, though, I received a call from Fluornoy saying his pilot had wrecked the Bell, and I didn't need to keep my appointment. A few days later he called again to say he was having trouble getting his Bell repaired and didn't care about doing it, and asked if I wanted to get in the helicopter business to take over a contract he had with local radio stations to provide traffic reports.

"What's it going to cost," I asked.

"Just the cost of a helicopter," Fluornoy replied.

I figured it might not be a bad idea if we could make some money. In speaking with a helicopter salesman, Wayne McKenzie of Alva, Oklahoma, the subject came up as to whom I could get to be the primary helicopter pilot. Wayne recommended a qualified young man named Ray Rowhuff, who was serving as a helicopter pilot in the Kansas Guard. To interview with me, he flew to Rawdon Airfield from Topeka, where he lived. Though Ray was not rated to give instruction or fly fixed-wing aircraft, his attitude, apparent energy, recommendations and Guard experience convinced me to offer him a job. His flight ratings could be gained while working at Aero Services. Ray accepted my offer only after flying back to Topeka and discussing the matter with his wife.

It was late November or early December by the time Ray relocated to Wichita and we had purchased a used helicopter. Ray started flying the radio air traffic reporters around, but because he still lacked an instructor's license, he couldn't give lessons, which limited the income the helicopter could produce. Ray brainstormed about ways to use the aircraft, hitting on an idea to fly into small towns to bring Santa Claus to Christmas parades and other festivities. Bad weather did not dissuade Ray from taking one flight to Alva, Oklahoma, though it should have. The turbulence caused Ray and Santa Claus to make a crash landing. They escaped with minor injuries, but the helicopter suffered a fair amount of damage. With mainly his spirits hurt, Ray worried about calling me to report the accident, because he was a new employee who had just wrecked a newly acquired expensive piece of equipment. The fact that my first question to him was whether anyone was hurt let him know his job wasn't in danger. The helicopter ended up being repaired and put back into service. Ray stayed with Aero Services for about a decade, gaining all his flight ratings and eventually taking charge of the company's flight operations.

SANTA DOWNED — Santa Claus, sometimes known as James Hitchcock, 32, Enid, Okla., suffered minor injuries Friday when this helicopter was flipped over by strong wind at Enid. Santa was in the 'co a it was landing at the Enid airport. — (Correspondent Photo.)

While flying Santa Claus to Oklahoma in the 1960s, new Aero Services pilot Ray Rowhuff lost control of a helicopter and crashed. He redeemed himself and later became director of flight operations for my business.

A couple of days before Christmas 1967, an East Saint Louis aircraft dealer named Jim Spurgeon contacted me to say he had a client interested in buying a twin-engine plane in my possession if I would take the client's single-engine Cessna as a trade-in. While preparing the twin-engine for takeoff, I was approached by one of the guys who hung out at Rawdon who said he'd always wanted to fly one. The man was in Wichita working a local construction job and had taken flight lessons at Rawdon in addition to spending spare time there, so I offered to let him come along and pilot the plane. On arrival, Jim, my guest and I spent a night on the town, and went to bed very late. Jim ran his operation out of a mobile home in which he also lived, and he let my guest and me stay the night there. I was to meet Jim's client at 9 a.m. at another nearby airport.

It was very cold that night, and Jim and the guy decided to warm up the plane the next morning to save me some time. I awoke to hear the engine running, and realized what they were doing, but before I could dress they had actually taken off. They returned in the Cessna 182, and told me what happened. After getting the plane warmed up, they decided to take care of the delivery and let me sleep. Jim thought my pilot had a multi-engine rating because he saw him fly the plane in. After they had taken off, Jim, who was not certified to fly a twin-engine, tried to turn over the controls to my pilot, who said, "I don't have a multi-engine rating." They decided to pilot the plane together, figuring that if they each took care of an engine they'd be OK.

I used similar logic on another occasion to play a small prank. After delivering a single engine plane somewhere in exchange for a twin-engine Piper Apache, I approached the flight line worker readying the plane and said to him, "I have single-engine certification; do you think I would be OK if I flew the Apache on just one engine?" He looked at me suspiciously, but didn't say I couldn't. Continuing my bluff, I entered the plane, started one engine and taxied off. The lineman ran into the service building to sound an alert about me. The people inside nearly reached the point of contacting the control tower before an acquaintance of mine let them in on the joke.

A large part of Aero Services' customer base came to be made of repeat and contracted clients. Forty years later, a number of them still stick in my mind. Providing flight time for students in the Wichita State University ROTC program is something I remember because we served them for about seven years. Sales calls ranged from doctors and politicians to farmers. Sometimes they came to Rawdon Field and sometimes my salesmen and I flew around the state to cultivate business in rural areas. For instance, we had a number of customers in Stanton County, on the Kansas-Colorado border, at the time the wealthiest county in the state on a per capita basis because of the large amount of irrigated acreage, which was highly appraised. Chief among them was Buell Scott, a farmer, irrigation equipment dealer and former significant state legislator who was in his seventies. After a period of time, Scott decided he liked his Mooney so much, he would sign up to be a dealer. Aero Services benefited greatly from the customer network Scott had built up through his other business ventures.

There were times when customers liked our planes enough they wouldn't let a poor sales pitch stop them from making the purchase. I received a call from a farmer who had been visited several times by one of my salesmen, the extremely likable Max Connor, who was unable to close the deal. "Rip, you've got to come out here and sell me a plane! All Max is doing is talking my ear off," the farmer said. Max and I flew out, and within ten minutes I had closed the deal by narrowing down why the farmer and his wife hesitated buying the plane: She wanted her husband's plane to be blue instead of red, to match his farm machinery and vehicles. Max was a retired teacher and flight enthusiast whom I thought showed potential, and he sold some planes but he mainly liked to visit with people and didn't always know how or when to close a deal.

The training I received to sell appliances for McKissack Brothers in post-World War II Tennessee never went out of date: Present the information the customer needs to make a decision and then wait for the customer to talk, to say what they like or don't like, then address their issues and make the deal. During my aircraft sales career, three deals stand out – the most profitable, the easiest, the most unusual.

My most profitable aircraft transaction involved two planes, neither of which I ever laid eyes on. In a sale generated by Jack Chastain, a pilot for the Petrolite Company of St. Louis, whom I knew when he was a test pilot for the Rawdon brothers, I traded a straight-from-the-factory Mooney MU2G for a Beech Model 18, which I sold to my former flight instructor, Nathan Sams, in Oklahoma. The Mooney Company delivered the MU2G to Petrolite, and Nathan went to Petrolite to pick up the Beech. I've always taken pride in my hard work, but I'm also proud that the most money I ever made with an aircraft transaction didn't involve much effort on my part.

The easiest deal I ever closed was with a customer from Sumner County,

Kansas, who had never owned a plane. He heard good things about Mooney aircraft and came to Rawdon Airfield for a demonstration flight. I took the man up and demonstrated the high performance of the plane at altitude and then the general ease of handling during takeoff and landing. It was a very hot day, and in the confined space of the Mooney, we both started to feel the heat after several takeoffs and landings. I ended the demonstration and moved discussion of the purchase to my office. After covering the sale and conditions with the customer and making up a contract, he viewed the information. I waited for his next comment. His started talking, "I really like that airplane, the performance was great. But, you know, it was hot during the takeoffs and landings. Did you notice I was sweating like a nigger–" The customer realized what he said and apologized profusely, explaining how unprejudiced he was.

I interrupted him, "Mister, if you were prejudiced, you wouldn't be buying this plane from me. Now here's a pen so we can finish up signing this contract." And he signed immediately. Later on, he invited me to his home and I met his family and found him to be a very open-minded and unprejudiced individual.

As for my most unusual sale, one day a very young-looking man and woman showed up at my agency expressing a desire to purchase a used plane I had in stock. They actually looked like they were still in high school, but I immediately proceeded to give them a demonstration in the plane they'd shown interest in.

After a short demo flight, before I had a chance to make a sales pitch, the young man said he was ready to buy the plane. I wrote the contract and he signed. While we readied the plane, he and his lady left for lunch, saying that he would be paying with a check and would leave his home banker's phone number in Alva, Oklahoma, so we could verify it. My office manager was excited when the banker told her that if the check was written for several times that amount, it would still be very much accepted. The young man turned out to be a very wealthy landowner who would later become a rancher in Wyoming. When he returned from lunch and took the plane, he said his first flight would be across town to Mid-Continent Airport to show his new purchase to an Aero Services competitor whose sales people had ignored him.

* *

During my years in Wichita I sold aircraft to very few African-Americans. To my recollection there were only six, excluding dealers: Tex Butler, C. Alfred "Chief" Anderson and Col. John Hicks (who bought a plane together), Chester Lewis and FAA inspector Lawrence Gonzalez (who also bought a plane together), and a doctor from Baltimore named Tom Jones.

Thirty years after Dr. Tom Jones bought a Mooney from me, he shows off a photo of the plane at his Florida home.

In the late 1960s, Tom happened across some information about me in an aviation trade magazine. He had been wanting to buy a Moone, and the opportunity to buy one from another African-American appealed to him, so he called me to order an airplane equipped to his specifications. Tom and his wife flew to Wichita and then flew with me to Mooney's Kerrville, Texas, base, where I spent the next several days teaching Tom to operate his new aircraft. He and I maintained occasional contact, and when I took a trip in 2000 to Florida, where the Joneses had retired, I spent the night with them. Tom proudly showed me a framed picture of the Mooney he'd bought from me decades earlier. Even though he'd sold the plane years before, he still kept a place for it in his heart!

As an FAA pilot examiner for twenty-eight years, I certified several thousand people for their licenses and almost daily one will see me somewhere and say hello. Once as I boarded an airline flight, the pilot spotted me. After he informed the passengers that the plane would likely encounter some thunderstorms and turbulence, he said he would try to give them the best ride he could because the guy who certified him to fly was on board.

My status came in handy for a pilot friend in the 1980s. I was driving on the Kansas Turnpike when I noticed a plane parked on the side of the highway, with a police officer and the pilot standing next to it. It had run out of gas and made an emergency landing. I pulled over and as I walked to the plane I heard the officer tell the pilot, "You're going to have to wait for the FAA to say you can put gas in this." The pilot saw me and said, "Here is the FAA right here! Is there any reason why I can't put gas in this thing?"

"I don't see why not," I said. As an examiner, I had no authority, but did not indicate that to the officer. My appearance saved my friend from waiting for an FAA inspector to show up.

Most pilot examinations are routine, without much to distinguish one from another, but a local pilot I see on occasion often tells about his experience with me. As part of his flight evaluation I assigned him to turn the plane 720 degrees around a point. He started the turn and noticed a car with a convertible top parked under us with a couple of people in it. I noticed that throughout the turn he kept losing altitude, and I asked him why.

"Do you see what I see?" he asked, and he started turning the plane the opposite direction so my side of the aircraft could provide me a view of the situation. Even with our altitude I could see the couple in the car making out. "Do you care if I descend now?" the pilot asked.

I didn't purposefully look for such situations, but some instructors looking for fun would have their students fly over a nudist camp near Hutchinson, Kansas. But that's another story.

* *

Bill Nichols, who owned a Honda motorcycle dealership on Wichita's West Douglas Avenue, became a flight student of mine because he wanted to decrease the amount of time he spent commuting from Wichita to a boat he kept in Marathon Beach, Florida. He liked water and if he had any spare time, he wanted to be with his boat.

His wife said that if he was learning to fly, she was too, so Aero Services started training both. When Bill obtained his private pilot license in 1970, he decided he was ready to buy a plane so he wouldn't need to schedule a rental. He didn't know what he wanted, so I showed him some used planes, and he found one that fit his bill. "What's it going to take to buy that plane?" he asked.

I gave him my price.

Now, we're two sales people who know how to negotiate. Bill calls one day and says, "Well, I want to buy that airplane, but I want to do it for a price I think is fair." He made me a counter offer.

"Bill, I can't take that. You started flying with us and I wanted you aboard as a customer, so I made you a special price to get you started."
A day or two later, Bill calls again, "You decide to take that offer?"

"No, I told you."

"Tell you what I'm going to do, I'm going to buy that plane from you." He made another offer.

"Bill, I told you what I wanted, and that's what I'm going to get for that plane. I made you my bottom-dollar offer because I wanted you as a customer."

"But, I'm going to be keeping my plane there at Rawdon, and getting gas and service there!"

"I put all that in when I made you the price," I said.

Another day or so later, Bill called. He'd gotten with someone who knew how to shop through a plane-sales magazine, that listed used aircraft. "I have a guy in Denver with a plane just like the one you want to sell me. He'll sell for a much lower price. But he's in Denver, and you're here and I still want to buy a plane from you. If you'll just meet me halfway between what he wants and you want, I'll buy from you."

"You're my friend, and I gave you my rock-bottom price."

"That guy's plane is just like the one you got."

"A used plane is a used plane," I said. "They're all different. Now, you've seen mine - if you want it, buy it."

Later in the afternoon, Bill called back to say the man from Denver was ready to fly his plane out to Rawdon to sell it the next day. "I'm still going to be your customer, but I want to double-check that you won't negotiate before I call him to fly out."

"I made you my last deal."

The next day, the plane never showed up at the appointed time, and Bill got restless. The Denver man said he'd had a conflict but would send a pilot out the next day. And so he did.

The plane came within radio contact and Bill, who was standing in my office, let everyone there know that was his plane. It started to land, and Bill said again, "That's my plane!" It taxied in, and Bill and the rest of us could see the thing leaking oil and looking battered. The pilot ambled in and asked if Mr. Nichols was there, "I've just flown his plane in."

"That ain't my airplane!" Bill said.

The pilot, a soldier on leave, told Bill he needed to go to Mid-Continent to catch a flight to his base in Nashville. "But you need to take that plane back to Colorado!" Bill said.

After Bill got the situation straightened out, he came in and apologized to me, "Rip, I made an ass out of myself. Forgive me!"

He eventually bought three more planes from me, all brand new.

Bill was really a nice guy. Throughout our business dealings, he would often invite my family to Marathon Beach, but the arrangement didn't work out until he bought his last plane from me. The plane was a twin-engine Aerostar, and Bill didn't have a multi-engine rating. He decided he'd rather spend time training in Marathon than Wichita, so he again extended his offer for a family vacation. "You can bring the wife and kids, and we'll fish and have a good time for a week, and get me my multi-engine rating," Bill said.

From left: Lawyer Walt Sawhill, my son Kerry, wife Augusta, me, and Bill Nichols in front of a plane he bought from me - the last of several.

The exotic vacation was well worth the wait. I hadn't been fishing in a long time, and my experience at Marathon Beach spoiled me so much that I haven't fished much since. My son, Kerry, who was 5, caught his first fish there and Bonita, who was 14, caught a barracuda that scared Augusta; "Bring it in!"

From left: My wife Augusta, daughter Bonita, son Kerry and I on the boat of motorcycle dealer Bill Nichols at Marathon Beach, Florida. Nichols offered to sponsor a family vacation if I delivered a plane and gave him lessons.

Bill encouraged her.

Bill's attorney, Walt Sawhill, also went with us, and tried to convince me to scuba dive. He would dive down and look at some coral, and tell me how beautiful it was, but Augusta said I wasn't about to go in that water after we'd just thrown Bonita's barracuda back into it.

"If you just put your head in the water, you can see the difference in the scenery of the coral," Walt said.

He was right; the view was beautiful. But I took my head back out of that water pretty quickly, lest I cross paths with that barracuda.

Bonita's barracuda

After finishing Bill Nichols' multi-engine training, my family prepared to go to the nearby Bahamas, to attend a Negro Airmen International convention, July 3-6, 1970, and Bill lent us his plane to make the brief trip.

The gathering include many of my old teachers from Tennessee, Tuskegee Experiment alumni and other black aviators, about 200 in all.

Between convention activities we shopped and visited the beach and casino. Additionally, my family got to meet the people who became important to me during the early part of my life, such as Tuskegee's "Chief" Anderson, who was honored by the Bahamian government and press for being the first to land a plane on the island of Nassau three decades before, and Perry Young, who gave me my first flying lesson. I spent some time playing golf with and renewing an acquaintance with Gen. Daniel "Chappie" James Jr., the first black four-star general in the Air Force. Based on this, he later helped me to sort out some trouble with a government contract. He told me, "There's a number of people who call themselves 'Rip,' but when you want an immediate answer from me, make sure to say it's Rip Gooch calling."

C. Alfred "Chief" Anderson plays with a trinket while former Tuskegee flight instructor Charlie Foxx and I watch during a 1971 NAI conference in Barbados.

When we flew into Nassau, Bahamas, I was the second of the airmen to land. I asked the airport service person if any other black pilots had flown in. He apparently didn't understand what I wanted to know. He said no, but seemed puzzled. I told him there'd be a lot of black pilots flying in because we were having a black pilots meeting.

I went to the hotel where we scheduled the meeting and checked in my wife and family and I went to sit by the swimming pool and have a highball. By happenstance, I met someone with whom I would have a long acquaintance, Horace Noble. He was in the pool with his daughter, and I sat next to his wife at poolside and started visiting about the meeting.

About that time, a couple of Bahamians came over and asked my name and if I had just flown in. I said I had, and they said they wanted to talk with me - in private. They took me into an office at the hotel and started quizzing me, eventually revealing that they would like me to leave the island. I questioned them somewhat, but they continued to insist that I leave.

"Why?" I asked.

"We don't want any trouble here," they said.

"What makes you assume that I'd create any trouble?"

"Well, we understand that you've flown in here and are going to be meeting with a lot of Black Power people."

When that came out, I realized there had been a mistake in my communication with the lineman at the airport. "Black pilots," of course, had been misunderstood as "Black Power." I insisted my questioners get in touch with the Bahamian minister of transport, who had invited the black pilots to the island. The problem was quickly resolved, but over the years my fellow Negro Airmen have often reminded me of my Black Power trip.

With some pioneers in black aviation, from left: Me, Cecil Ryan (flight instructor for the Tuskegee Airmen, later head of aviation at Tennessee State University), C. Alfred "Chief" Anderson (the father of black aviation) and Perry Young (the first black airline pilot).

—*Reflections*—

Banker Earl Chandler assisted Aero Services in obtaining loans during its early years, and also became a flight student and customer of my business. Years later he recognized one of my old Mooney aircraft somewhere and photographed the occasion.

Chapter 24
The World of Banking

I had met Jerry Brindell in the 1960s when he worked as a manufacturing representative for Chrysler. He had an interest in flying and came to Rawdon Field for lessons. By 1971 he was serving as an aide to Kansas Gov. Robert Docking. Jerry called me one January day to ask if I would approve of the governor appointing me as a Wichita representative on the Kansas Civil Rights Commission. I had never met Docking, so I wondered if Jerry recommended me.

"I'm busy with my government contracts and aircraft sales," I told Jerry. "I don't mind helping others get into office, but I don't have any interest in getting a position myself, much less one that doesn't pay."

"Often, Rip, people who do this find an issue that they can benefit from just by serving," he said.

I chose to serve the four-year term, and found that Jerry was correct. In addition to working alongside active, well-intended people, I took pride in helping improve minority opportunities and relations in the community and the state.

Later, in 1973, while riding home from a Kansas Office of Minority Business Enterprise (KANOMBE) meeting in Hutchinson with Dr. Othello Curry, we discussed the lack of capital available from white-owned banks to help minorities and minority businesses. It was a topic we often discussed when he would fly with me to far-away KANOMBE meetings, or when I rode with him to near ones, but it was on that ride from Hutchinson that we decided to form our own bank to help solve that problem.

Dr. Curry and I formulated a list of possible individuals who could invest money in forming the bank. I used my connections with the Kansas Civil Rights Commission to call the governor's office for some guidelines on establishing a bank. Jerry Brindell recommended finding a lawyer who knew how to develop a banking charter, saying that the governor (who was a banker himself) and others would back the bank's formation if the paperwork was completed and filed properly.

Changes in investors, lawyers and proposed locations became a problem, and the Kansas Banking Commission was losing patience with the University State Bank. We charter investors were approaching the deadline for filing a fourth application when our lawyer, Al Kamus, struck a deal to receive financial assistance from the Kansas State Bank and a professional investor, R. Dee Hubbard. With that, the University State Bank opened on the southwest corner of 17th Street and Hillside, across an intersection from Wichita State University. The area was, and is, mostly populated by minorities.

The University Bank doubled its investors' money by 1979. At about that time, the majority stockholder, investor and entrepreneur, Hubbard, decided he wanted to sell his share. Hubbard, a white, had been brought into our bank charter initially because we couldn't find any more minorities to invest. He agreed to keep his money with us until the bank was on its feet,

Wilbert Johnson, Vice President

The real reason success?

The University State Bank's Family - L. to R., Back row (partially obscured) is Rochelle Parker, Teller; Joyce Bobbitt, New Accounts; Julie Williams, Teller; Teretha Lewis, Asst. Cashier; (front row) Meta Title, Secretary; Kathy Gilhausen, Teller; Glenda Cates, Teller; Sue Kennedy, Executive Secretary; and Bank Guard Jim Bryant. Other employees not shown are Clynita Woods, Supervisor, Accounting Department; Theresa Yates, Accounting Department and Sylvia Oliver, Accounting Department.

Wichita Times April 8, 1976

Employees of the University State Bank, the first and only minority-owned bank in Wichita, Kansas, which I helped charter. It was located near Wichita State University.

at which point we could buy it or find someone to buy his share and he'd sell it at a fair price.

He gave the rest of us time to find a new partner, but no one in the community wanted to pay market value for it. They wanted to buy in for the same price the original investors had spent several years earlier. Some of the people talked to their own bankers, who told them not to get involved. Some were influenced by their families, who didn't understand business. A couple of people we spoke with had small businesses but couldn't grasp the concept. The owners of mom-and-pop hot dog stands often think of a bank as someplace to borrow money rather than as an investment.

Ultimately, Hubbard sold to a local banking group that then sold to another banking group from Hutchinson, headed by a man named Marty Burke. Shortly after that, Burke bought out all the other original investors except me. In the time it took for these deals to be made, the return on the shareholders' money had decreased slightly, to one and a half times the initial investment. I figured we were still growing, and the investment would bounce back. I was very wrong.

Though, the bank opened an additional branch by 1982 - at 21st and Oliver streets, one of Wichita's busiest intersections - Burke spread the bank's money too thin with other dealings. He funneled money into a variety of major investments that were unsuccessful, some mortuaries and real estate in Wichita, California and elsewhere. His strategy caused the bank to run out of money. I tried to recruit depositors and accounts in the community, but Marty was making loans outside the state and community and taking most of the assets.

One bank purchase was a piece of real estate a mile east of the University Bank's 21st Street branch, at 21st and Woodlawn. The land was expensive then and has increased in value exponentially; there was talk of building a new main bank location on it. Somehow the land deed was filed as Burke's personal property. When the bank failed soon after, the 21st and Woodlawn lot did not sell with the bank's holdings but remained with Burke, who made a sizable profit upon selling it.

After resolving my problem with the IRS over Aero Services' debt, I, along with the other bank partners, was now faced with owing the federal banking commission. It took over the bank and sold it and its liabilities and if there'd been enough remaining, we partners would get what was leftover, but there was nothing leftover. The insurance paid off the depositors. Bank IV ended up buying the University Bank as cheaply as it could, for pennies on the dollar.

Despite its failure, the bank succeeded during its life, among other dealings, in financing the building of an American Legion club in the city's black area and assisting in establishing a locally based minority cross-country bus company. The University Bank was historically significant on a local level as Wichita's first minority-owned, minority oriented bank.

—*Reflections*—

From left: son Kerry, daughter Camille, wife Augusta, granddaughter Dorian, me, daughter Bonita, and Air Force Major Ed Andrews, who was like a second son.

Chapter 25
Family

In May 1960, during Aero Services' very early days, I flew to Chicago to visit my sister Christine, who had been admitted to a hospital for a heart condition. Though we were never a regular physical presence in each other's lives, Christine and I maintained a strong emotional bond since my childhood, when she often cared for me in my mother's absence on the Scott farm. Visiting her in the hospital, I thought she'd recover soon. Weeks later, in early June, she was still there when I took an overnight trip to Moline, Illinois, with a businessman who had just bought his first plane and couldn't fly alone. I had a gut feeling I should make time to stop in Chicago to see Christine. When the businessman and I returned to Rawdon Airport on June 8, the first message waiting for me said Christine had died. Two years later she was followed by Aunt Lula, whose death was not so sudden. Aunt Lula's health had declined fairly steadily for several years, and I moved her from Tennessee to Wichita to live with my family so we could take care of her. She knew Wichita would be the last place she would live, and she expressed concern that she wouldn't be able to be buried in Tennessee next to Uncle Fred. I promised her we would fly her body home when the time came. Later, as she lay in her deathbed, she said, "You have done all you can for me, and I am proud of you."

Those words meant a lot to me, coming from the woman who had served as my mother figure for so long. As the wife of a sharecropper, she had never led a very comfortable existence, and I took great joy in caring and providing for Aunt Lula. When she passed, I called my former flying instructor, Nathan Sams, who owned a flight operation in Muskogee, Oklahoma, and he provided and piloted the plane that took Aunt Lula home.

In building Aero Services I sacrificed much family time. Christine's and Aunt Lula's deaths helped me realize I had to make the most of the times I was able to spend with Augusta and my daughters. As a result, once in awhile we took extended weekend jaunts to a variety of locales: Chicago, Las Vegas, Colorado, Mexico. Sometimes, when I had to attend meetings of organizations I belonged to, such as the Negro Airmen International, I'd pack up the family to go with me. Bonita and Camille enjoyed casually visiting places that their school friends could see only on real vacations. These family excursions often went smoothly because I had made contacts or friends in the places where we planned to go, and the girls still think of me as knowing everyone everywhere.

Our family also expanded during this time, with a son, Kerry Lee Gooch, who joined us February 27, 1965. Though he was born prematurely, weighed less than two pounds and spent his first three months in the hospital, he grew up normally and became a robust high school football player. Kerry was able to hold on to my aircraft controls before he could walk, often falling asleep with his hands on them. I can't say whether he was born to fly, but he spent enough time sitting in my lap that he picked up on a lot of learning that likely led to him eventually choosing a career in aviation. The success Aero Services was enjoying at the time of his birth allowed me to spend more time at home; Augusta and I would joke that she raised Camille and Bonita and I raised Kerry.

My family, clockwise from top left: children Bonita, Kerry and Camille, wife Augusta and me around 1980.

My father enjoyed holding Kerry on his only visit to Kansas in 1967. My dad wouldn't fly so I drove him. He also spent most of his visit in our guest room because he missed his two room cabin and outhouse. Frank had changed greatly since my time in the military. He gave up alcohol cold turkey sometime in the 1940s. I went to visit him and I was about to drink some bourbon, when he noticed and said to give the bottle to him; he threw it away. He must have considered what liquor did to him, and what it might do to me. Never again did I drink in his presence, not even a beer. Though he did not become a regular churchgoer, he reached a spiritual reckoning in his life

In his later years, when he could watch baseball on television, he found it very exciting. He spent time sitting in Nutbush general store visiting with other codgers. If I was flying through that way, I would detour and circle over his house. People commented to me about how proud he was telling them that was his boy flying up there. He was relieved to think that I wasn't wasting my life the way he wasted his. My dad died in February 1972.

My daughter Camille's wedding party included two young men bound for success. My son Kerry (front right) became a pilot and neighbor Barry Sanders (left of Kerry, as ring bearer) became an NFL football star.

By the end of 1967, we faced another change with Camille finishing high school and leaving home for college. Even though we lived four blocks from Wichita State University, she said she definitely was not going there. She said she was moving out, even if it meant just going to Emporia State University, a couple of hours north of Wichita, which she did for two years before transferring to Pittsburg State in eastern Kansas, where she obtained an accounting degree. Through a job placement company Camille was hired a position with General Electric in Milwaukee, Wisconsin, where she found the weather was not to her liking. "It's my last year in Milwaukee in the winter!" she said on a visit home. Soon after, again through the job placement company, she relocated to Dallas to work with Collins Radio Corporation, married a young man she met in her apartment complex, and, in 1978, provided Augusta and me with our first grandchild, a girl named Dorian. Camille and her husband eventually divorced and she is currently living in Atlanta with Dorian, who has a master's degree in business administration and works for Coca-Cola.

My daughter Bonita, far left, was a University of Kansas cheerleader.

Bonita, meanwhile, went to Fort Worth for her first job after graduating from the University of Kansas in the mid-1970s. Her bachelor's degree was in communication, but after interning at a local TV station, she decided she wasn't going to be happy there and returned to KU for a master's degree in public administration. While Bonita worked on her master's degree, a former Wichita friend of mine, Vernell Sturns, who had become city manager of Fort Worth, called me to see if Bonita would be interested in interviewing for a job with him. She won the job, and within six months of living in Texas decided to marry. She wanted a wedding that would be considered extravagant by middle-class standards. I was hesitant and so was Augusta, but she was easy for Bonita to sway because her own wedding had been very modest. Augusta rented a banquet hall for the reception and, for the singer hired former Ink Spots member Johnny Harris, whom Bonita had seen perform in a local nightclub. In a few years, Bonita and her husband moved to West Palm Beach, Florida, and she accepted a job as an assistant to the city manager of Riviera Beach. By the time she became a full-fledged assistant city manager in Del Rey Beach, her marriage had ended. In the mid-1990s she moved back to Wichita to own and operate the city's black newspaper, The Community Voice, and raise my second granddaughter, Lauren.

Each of my daughters was so closely associated with my aviation business that they didn't have a great interest in flying, even though they took lessons and soloed near their sixteenth birthdays. They had to wait until 16 due to FAA age guidelines. Kerry, though, loved flying and at the age of 12 decided he was going to solo before he hit 16. There was no getting around the regulations, but we found a way to pacify him. He started on gliders and soloed on those at 14, and continued to build ratings as guidelines allowed, up to soloing in a fixed-wing aircraft at 16 and becoming an instructor at 18.

One of my son's early Christmases; it was much different from those of my childhood.

I thought Kerry's future in aviation would be unlimited, because times had changed significantly since I started flying. I saw him as on the move, a very motivated young man. During his senior year of high school I bought him a Cessna 172. He said that when he turned 18 and gained his instructor rating he would use the plane to earn money to pay for college by giving lessons. Right out of Wichita Heights High School he attended Wichita State University - and flunked out. He wasn't challenged there, having already gained all his flight certifications and more aviation knowledge than the people around him. He was giving lessons, as he intended, but he would also take off with girls for weekends in Dallas, not returning until the middle of the next week. He found himself at a loss for what he was going to do for the long term.

Kerry showed up one day with an idea that he was going to go to the military and have it pay for his college flight training. He went into an Air National Guard unit and failed the color-blind portion of the physical required to enter flight school. He was then sent to aircraft mechanic training school for nine months, and came home with a different look at life. The military time did a lot to strengthen his character and motivate him. With a part-time job with a local aircraft parts manufacturer during the week, he spent weekends in the Guard. We spoke about what he was going to do for his education. Central Missouri State University in Warrensburg seemed to be a good choice. I had been impressed by the campus when I previously traveled there as a guest speaker for a summer aviation class, and one of the instructors was, Tom Hemphill, a former business associate at Aero Services. He had known Kerry from birth, and I knew Tom would serve as a good role model.

Soon after Kerry and I returned to Wichita from a campus visit and a meeting with the head of the CMS aviation department, Tom called, saying there was a major problem. Kerry couldn't enter the university due to flunking out at WSU. Tom recommended Kerry spend the summer getting good grades in easy classes at nearby Butler County Community College, and then CMS would accept him in the fall. Kerry enrolled in dancing or physical education, received good grades and forwarded those to Missouri. Starting in fall 1986, his third year out of high school, Kerry went to CMS straight through for three years, obtaining both his undergraduate and master's degrees. Following his August 1989 graduation with a master's degree in aviation management, he immediately went to work in marketing for Beech Aircraft, the first African-American to work there in a position that required the worker to be a pilot.

My son Kerry's graduation from Central Missouri State University with a master's degree thrilled the family because he had flunked out of Wichita State only a few years before, due to hard partying. From left: My daughters Bonita and Camille, granddaughter Dorian, Kerry, wife Augusta, and me.

Augusta and I had been married for more than twenty years by the early 1970s, and we had rarely spent time by ourselves. We both worked constantly. Fortunately, we were able to rekindle our love. Early in 1971, I decided to take a Dale Carnegie self-empowerment course, and Augusta joined me. The Carnegie courses focus on strengthening relationships, handling stress, solving problems and being persuasive, among other things, and I was very surprised that Augusta was interested. For the first time, we were put in a classroom together, engaging in activities that were very different from our usual husband-wife roles. The twelve weekly sessions caused us to be competitive with each other, and put more passion in our relationship. By the time we graduated from the course in April 1971, we came to know each other much better than we had, and grew much closer.

That same year, for a Negro Airmen International convention, Augusta and I traveled to Barbados by ourselves and had just as wonderful a time as the year prior in Florida with Bill Nichols and in the Bahamas with NAI. With no set schedule, the only thing we had to focus on was enjoying ourselves, which was easy to do in Barbados because the environment there was not as fast paced as in the Bahamas, Kingston or Nassau. On the way home we spent a few days in New York, where we went anywhere we felt like going, such as to see the United Nations building or to see what Harlem was really like.

A vacation to Barbados with my wife helped rekindle passion in our relationship.

Every other time that we had gone someplace together, somebody would recognize and greet me, but Augusta thought I could escape that in the Big Apple. As we walked into the Empire State Building, however, I was spotted by TWA pilot Kemp Talley and his wife, Dolores, whom he'd met while stationed at Wichita's McConnell Air Force Base. Augusta rolled her eyes!

Flying home from a 1982 Negro Airmen International fly-in at Tuskegee gave us another story. Augusta and I decided to fly to Nashville for a night and then possibly attend that year's World's Fair in Knoxville. As we took off at Tuskegee, the gear of our Mooney wouldn't go up, but I succeeded in raising it part-way after several tries. I didn't mention anything to Augusta because I thought I would be able to put the gear down manually when we arrived in Nashville. Prior to our flight I had noticed that some bad weather would be moving into Nashville at about the time of our arrival, but I thought we could beat it. The weather was about to reach the city as Augusta and I approached the airport. I tried to lower the gear, but it was still jammed. I radioed the tower about the problem and was told to pull out of the traffic pattern and continue attempting to lower the gear. After breaking the gear handle, I had no choice but to do a gear-up landing. Air traffic controllers asked me to pass by the tower for them to double-check the situation, and I made sure they got a good close-up look. They yelled, "It's not down!"

I requested permission to land with the gear up, but the controllers wanted to give me help on how to possibly lower the gear. I informed them that they would be hard pressed to find anyone with more experience in a Mooney than me; I just wanted to land, and I said I wanted to land on grass (landing on the concrete would have ruined the bottom of my plane). The airport manager was put on the radio and said I'd be landing at my own risk. By this time, fire trucks, an ambulance and the media had arrived on the airfield. I landed on the grass parallel to the runway, ending up near a fire truck. "Good landing," someone said. Augusta and I escaped unhurt.

When we arrived at our airport hotel room, I called some friends to visit us. The manager, who was also an old friend, sent up a bottle of booze. I turned the television to the local news broadcast, and one of the top stories was about a small plane crashing at the airport, with no one being injured. Conversation turned to the crash, and I told our guests it was our plane. "No, the airplane that crashed," our guests said. "That was us," I said.

"You weren't in the airplane that crashed!" Our friends couldn't understand how Augusta and I could be so calm and collected. The next morning I reported the accident to the FAA, and the local official said he had all he needed to know and that he'd get hold of the news video: it could be used as training film for wheel-up landings.

With just Kerry living with us by the mid-1970s, Augusta and I decided the time had come to look for a new home. In 1979 we located a fairly large, mostly stone house near the northwest corner of 21st Street and Oliver, about a mile from the University Bank and also virtually across the street from Wichita State University. Part of the stone-and-wood house had been built when Oliver was a wagon road a few decades before, and over the years had been enlarged into a ranch-style affair. With its large lawn and accompanying trees, it reminded me of my farm childhood in Tennessee. On the Tennessee estate my family occupied a shack located on the lawn of the big house, one of three little shanties along the road. I was told I used to play out in the lawn, where there was a duck pond and grazing horses. I had often returned and looked at that place to get a feel for it, because I really wasn't old enough to have developed a memory of it by the time I left there at the age of four. My appreciation of the area's beauty, though, was always tempered by my memory of the shanties.

I once promised myself that if I became a millionaire I'd buy that big house in Tennessee; the house in Wichita appeared to be the next best thing. When I looked at the house on Oliver, fifty years after moving from the Scott farm, I saw owning it as my chance to be in the main house instead of the shanty, a constant source of satisfaction that I had accomplished something in life and elevated my family out of poverty. That the southern quarter of the house could be closed off as an apartment appealed to Kerry. There was a bedroom, office and, above, a workout area. Plus, he was about fourteen, an age where he didn't want to be around his parents very much, and his parents were getting to where they would rather he'd leave them alone, too. That clinched the deal.

I once promised myself that I would someday buy the big house on the farm where I was born. This home in north Wichita, Kansas - my current residence - reminded me of it, and had no shacks on its lawn.

Chapter 26
People, Places, Things

One of a number of flight organizations in which I maintained a long membership was Negro Airmen International. Its name is self-explanatory; it is the oldest of the black aviation associations that have developed since World War II, founded by Ed Gibbs, one of the most highly regarded civilian instructors with the Tuskegee flight program.

In 1971 at an informal gathering of some Negro Airmen International members, a longtime friendly rivalry resulted in organizing a new event that also became an annual tradition. Horace Noble of the Chicago chapter and Dr. Jesse Hayes of the Houston chapter decided to see which group had the most members who owned and flew airplanes. They designated the upcoming Memorial Day weekend to get as many aircraft as possible to fly to Yazoo City, Mississippi, which was somewhat equidistant between Chicago and Houston.

Horace Noble of Chicago (right) and Jesse Hayes of Houston two decades after they started Operation Skyhook.

Operation Skyhook, as they dubbed it, was set up as a fundraiser for the local Catholic and largely black St. Francis Parish and its Head Start school program. It is still debated among those pilots which group had the most fly in, but so many people showed up that we filled a whole motel in Yazoo and part of one in a nearby community. The town had no taxis, so the priest in charge arranged for the police to substitute as our taxi service. He also arranged for the pilots to take children for free flights. Some entertainment was provided by a former Tuskegee flight instructor, Matthew Plumber from Texas, who used his PT-17 for aerobatics while I narrated the performance. Hearkening back to my own air show days, I tried to work up the audience the same way that Bill Sweet had done for me, "And there he goes! Nobody is ever supposed to do that in an airplane!"

I emceed the aerobatics portion of the first Operation Skyhook in Yazoo City, Mississippi.

Aero Services hosted Operation Skyhook at Rawdon Airfield in 1972, but it was overshadowed by two tragedies, both involving pilots from Texas. En route to the event, Paul Brown of Dallas crashed and was killed near Mulvane, Kansas, several miles south of Wichita. Then, just before the Houston chapter president and I returned from identifying his body, Dr. Herman Barnett of Houston died in a crash at the end of the Rawdon runway.

Despite this situation, Wichita's Operation Skyhook was a success. Due to corporate sponsorship from companies such as Boeing, Beechcraft and Cessna, the black airmen enjoyed their stay and would return to Wichita for conventions of Negro Airmen International and similar organizations, and to several other national fly-ins hosted at Rawdon Airfield.

The corporate sponsorship was made possible through my association with

George Johnson, a highly decorated Army aviator who became a close friend. George was employed by Beechcraft, and used his contacts among Wichita's aviation companies to solicit help. One reason the aircraft companies supported the national meets was that we incorporated youth-oriented activities into the conventions to stimulate aviation interest among young people and expose them to professionals in the field. Often our outreach efforts allowed these youth to take their first flights in general aviation aircraft. In this way we tried to impart to them that this light-aircraft training was where a majority of airline pilots started out.

Aero Services by itself provided a good, consistent environment for aviators to learn the ropes. Part of this can be attributed to the function that small airports served as social centers for pilots, would-be pilots and just plain aviation enthu-siasts prior to the 1980s. If they weren't out flying or learning to fly, these hangers-on would sit around and talk about planes for hours. Some of the acquaintances and friends I gained from this setting were people I would not otherwise have associated with – doctors, lawyers, car dealers, and others. A number of these people became valuable to me in years to come, when I changed professions.

Because I, Aero Services' owner, was black, the small number of black pilots and enthusiasts in the Wichita area, some from the city's McConnell Air Force Base, gravitated to Rawdon Airfield. Watching out for my own, I tried to do what I could to advance these people's interests.

One unique time involved a former Army helicopter pilot, Bob Lawson, who had been accepted to enter airline pilot training with TWA. When he appeared for entry, it was noted that his pilot experience was on helicopter and he would need a fixed-wing commercial instrument rating before he could get in. Immediately he called me, and through accelerated effort I was able to provide him his rating and get him to TWA, where he became a pilot, joining a few other early blacks in the airline industry, to name a few: Kemp Talley, John Gordon, Paul Robinson, Jim Whitehead, Clarence Powell and Bennie Clay (who had also gotten his start at Rawdon Airfield). All these pilots retired from major airlines; some took other flying jobs, some – like Bob and Kemp – took to the golf course.

Other black pilots I helped found successful careers.

George Johnson, whose parents lived next door to the Water Street Cafe when Augusta ran it in the early 1950s, enlisted in the Army as a teenager and matured to win the Distinguished Flying Cross during the Vietnam War, the first black to win the honor during that conflict and one of the few

Army helicopter pilots to do so. When he retired from the military, he returned to Wichita. George took a job at Beech Aircraft and became the first black in a management position there. On retiring twenty-four years later, he started his own business, the Diversified Educational Training and Manufacturing Company, which I helped him set up.

Sol Skates was a petroleum engineer in Kansas City who struggled finding money enough to earn licenses and flight time. While I had an airplane sales office at the now defunct Fairfax Airport in Kansas City, Kansas, I made sure to give him every chance possible to fly on jobs for me. He was later hired by TWA.

As a youngster, Bob Johnson, a relative of mine from Lauderdale County, Tennessee, would watch me fly to a landing strip near his home when I visited Aunt Lula and Uncle Fred. Bob became a military helicopter pilot and later moved to Wichita and flew for Aero Services for a time. Now, he's one of the top oil-rig pilots around. When Hurricane Katrina ravaged New Orleans in 2005, Bob spent days before flying men and materials off the gulf's oil rigs, and days after surveying the damage.

High school students Bennie Clay and his brother Harold rode their bikes several miles from their home to Rawdon Airfield one day in 1959 to ask the cost for an hour of flight time, and put down a deposit of a pocketful of change. They returned the next week with another pocketful of change that didn't add up to the price, but I took them up anyway for an hour flight. They started hanging around the airport, took some lessons and later became airline pilots. Bennie battled racism at United Airlines and was then hired by TWA, while Harold flew for Air Midwest. Both are now retired.

Someone else who learned to fly at Rawdon Airfield was Air Force enlisted man Harold Sims, who went to Hollywood and performed air stunts in a number of movies. Other black pilots I employed but did not train included Claudell James, who flew for Aero Services early on, and Bill Turner, who piloted for Aero Services' under a military contract for work at Patuxent Naval Air Station in Maryland.

During my lifetime, I have made many acquaintances, but only a few of the thousand or more I've met have elevated themselves beyond the level of acquaintanceship and become my personal friends. Maybe none have become so close to me as former Air Force officer Ed Andrews. He grew to be like another son; I often have called him my god-sent child.

We first crossed paths when Aero Services operated a courier service for the government during the Vietnam War. I was constantly adding and replacing pilots, and I kept an eye out for minorities because I knew that majority companies wouldn't go out of the way to hire them. Someone told me about Ed, who lived in Florida and was instructing part time while looking for a full-time aviation job.

I called him to set up a meeting. I planned to attend a conference in Lake Geneva, Wisconsin, and would be glad to meet with him there to discuss his job opportunities. He impressed me very much during our meeting, and I had no trouble deciding that he would be good to work with. I left Lake Geneva thinking Ed would join Aero Services. A short while later he called to say he had been offered a piloting job near his home, and asked if I'd be disappointed if he took it. Of course I was disappointed, but I wished him well. Several years later, around 1975, Ed showed up as a 2nd lieutenant assigned to McConnell Air Force Base's missile wing.

We renewed our acquaintance over the five years he was stationed in Wichita, and Ed bonded with my son. Kerry was in his teenage years and looking for a big-brother role model, and Ed was there. Our whole family, in fact, became so bonded to Ed that we referred to him as a son and brother, and other people thought he was, too.

Ed's wife calls me "Pop," as my kids do, and his daughter refers to me as Grandpa Rip. After he retired from the military, I thought he'd return to aviation as a profession, but he didn't. He owns an automobile dealership in Kingsland, Georgia, and lives on a golf course, which comes in handy when I visit him.

Air Force Major Ed Andrews (right) came to be a big brother to my son Kerry (left). Here they are at my 40th wedding anniversary celebration in 1987.

—Reflections—

Celebrating Christmas with, from left, daughter Bonita, granddaughter Lauren, granddaughter Dorian, daughter Camille and grandson Kerry Jr.

Extended family: Ed Andrews with his wife, Rose, and daughter, Roshelle, in 2005.

Chapter 27
Government Contractor

Flower children and other picketers, black and white, stood around in front of buildings and monuments in the nation's capital. From inside our city bus we could hear them yelling, chanting, burning flags and, in general, making their case against the Vietnam War and/or racial inequality.

Along with about fifteen other businessmen from Kansas, I had been invited to Washington, D.C., in early 1969 for a national conference organized by Congress to develop and enact a plan to nurture relations between white-owned businesses and minority-owned businesses in hope that it would help the country heal as a whole from the effects of its discriminatory history.

Taking place three years after implementation of President Johnson's Economic Opportunity Loan Program, which assisted minorities in establishing their own businesses, the conference was one of the first efforts the federal government made toward addressing Black Power demands to provide work for those minority businesses. Following the public furor over the July 1967 Detroit race riot and the April 1968 assassination of Martin Luther King Jr., the government finally seemed to realize it had to try to actively empower blacks economically rather than just pass laws.

The conference delegations from every state were diverse, and efforts had been made to invite the most prominent and/or most promising business people and community leaders. Among the Kansas delegation were future Wichita construction magnate Jessie Cornejo, veterinarian Othello Curry, contractor Ron Skellen, realtor Floyd Pitts, oil man Henry Worford, Kansas City electric company owner Willie Ray Walker, and Wichita-based millionaire Willard Garvey, who was assigned to be leader of our group, despite being white. Garvey may even have had a hand in selecting which business people were to go to Washington.

The bus ride around the city disturbed us, as it was probably meant to. We entered the conference with a feeling of urgency to meet the goal we had been called to confront. As we situated ourselves in a Congressional conference room listening to the opening remarks a group of black radicals interrupted the proceedings, saying money, not talk, was needed for economic empowerment. They continued to interrupt to the point that it became apparent that nothing was going to be accomplished at the conference. The meeting was eventually discontinued, with the event's organizers deciding it would be best for each state's delegation to meet with its congressional representatives, brainstorm ways to boost minority business interests and relations with majority businesses, and then reconvene with the other states to present the ideas.

The delegations returned to their home states to form federally funded fact-finding groups to devise how the government could best provide work to minority-owned businesses. Because the feds couldn't dictate to public-sector businesses that they had to give a certain amount of work to minority-owned companies, the plan that developed involved the government itself awarding work contracts to minority businesses to get them on their feet and ready to compete against large businesses. Due to the Vietnam War, there was much government work available. The Small Business Administration was to administer two main programs to advance minority opportunities. The 7(a) program gave the government responsibility for providing guarantees against bank defaults on loans to minority businesses. Then, most importantly, the 8(a) program guaranteed that a certain percentage of government contracts would be awarded to minority businesses. With Executive Order 11458, President Nixon formed, through the U.S. Department of Commerce, the Office of Minority Business Enterprise to make sure the 7(a) and 8(a) programs were being administered correctly. Coincidentally, the Office of Minority Business Enterprise was headed by John Jenkins, a former schoolmate of mine from Tennessee State University who had gone on to law school and government work.

The Kansas delegation had returned to open a Kansas Office of Minority Business Enterprise in Topeka, the state capital, with branches later in Kansas City and Wichita. With the fact-finding completed, the Kansas Office of Minority Business Enterprise turned to holding meetings informing minority entrepreneurs of the opportunities available to them. It worked in an advisory capacity to identify what government work they could likely obtain contracts for, and directing them to the Small Business Administration, which matched contracts with contractors. Kansas' Rep. Garner Shriver, en. Bob Dole and their staffs became very helpful in appropriating funds and making government contacts available to companies in the region. Wichita-area SBA manager Deryl Schuster, who was white, tried his best to help minority operations, though he sometimes employed underlings who did not.

Aero Services became one of the first contractors involved in the 8(a) program, but we ran into some trouble. Though Aero Services was one of the only black aviation contractors in the country, the government offered very few contracts that fit the services available at Rawdon Field. The minority businesses that benefited most from the 8(a) program were maintenance oriented, cleaning government buildings. In contrast, Aero Services' main function was chartering, selling and maintaining aircraft. We couldn't build the jets being demanded for use in Vietnam, which precluded us from a manufacturing contract.

By late 1970, Wichita's general aviation economy had declined sharply, and Aero Services' cash flow had suffered. As I had done during other periods in my life, I adapted, but barely. In about two years Aero Services would have government contracts totaling about $353,000, an amount that allowed us to scrape by. The situation was made worse because we could have negotiated the contracts for much more had the Small Business Administration representative assigned to me been more helpful. On the bright side, the government work allowed me an opportunity to hire some minority pilots for their first regular flying jobs, and also provide business to other black aviation operations, such as Warren Wheeler Air Service in North Carolina, which helped us occasionally when planes were needed on an emergency basis.

Aero Services' air taxi service matched a negotiated government contract for a courier service to transport classified documents and materials. The contract required use of multiengine planes with two pilots per aircraft, who, along with related personnel, had to gain top-secret security clearance. In addition to the sometimes months-long waiting period to gain security clearance, to win the contract Aero Services also had to purchase a number of twin-engine Beechcrafts, as well as arrange for office space and living quarters near the military installations we covered in seventeen states. This included locations in Jacksonville, Florida; Omaha, Nebraska; and Charleston, South Carolina.

In addition to the courier contract, Aero Services won another contract to help test and

Aero Services used Beech Model 18s to transport classified government documents during the Vietnam War.

Aero Services used twin-engine Beechcrafts to fulfill government contracts to test flight equipment at a military base in Maryland.

evaluate experimental aircraft instruments at the Patuxent River Naval Air Station in Lexington Park, Maryland. The instrument equipment would be loaded into racks in an Aero Services plane and Naval personnel would operate and read the instruments while telling Aero Service pilots where and how to maneuver the aircraft to obtain the test results from the equipment. Fortunately, the aircraft required to fulfill the contract was the same that was needed for the courier service.

A third contract we received in November 1970 involved overhauling UH-1 Bell helicopter rotor hubs (the part that holds the blades), for which we had to custom-build machinery. Until that time, only the Bell Aircraft Corporation had overhauled worn-out hubs for its helicopters, which were being used in Vietnam. The first problem I encountered in winning the contract was that Bell was not interested in seeing any of its work go to another company. The second problem was that the equipment used for the final testing of the rotor hubs was unique to the Bell Corporation, which was not going to lend or sell anything to Aero Services.

The first problem could be overcome if we acquired the equipment to do the job, so we focused on solving the second problem. Through Garner Shriver and his staff I was able to visit an air base in Mississippi and see what would be required to overhaul and test the hubs. With me was my friend Glenn Stearman, who owned an aviation parts manufacturing business in the

Wichita suburb of Valley Center. He took note of what Bell's equipment did to test the hubs, and was able to make machinery to do the same job, though it was wholly his own design.

For a time during the Vietnam War, Aero Services overhauled Bell UH-1 helicopter rotor hubs under a contract obtained through the government's 8A minority business program.

We converted part of a building at Rawdon Field to accommodate the new operation, and reached the point that we had two shifts overhauling rotor hubs. Until Glenn completed building the test machine, we set the hubs aside to await testing. When the machine was finished, however, a third obstacle presented itself. The military's overhaul manual only authorized hubs that were marked as having final testing on Bell equipment, a situation that would prevent us from being paid and our hubs from being accepted for use. Inspectors came to look at our machine, and found that it filled the same testing requirements as Bell's; its only fault was its lack of name. After running a gamut of red tape and bureaucracy involving inspectors, politicians and generals (including Daniel "Chappie" James), Aero Services was successful in gaining government clearance under the condition that our testing machine was made to bear an identification plate designating it as a unique Aero Services machine. The overhaul manual was changed to read that hubs could be tested only on Bell or ASI equipment.

Despite the government approval, the Aero Services hubs were shipped off to a warehouse for storage, not intended for use, an official later told me. The military, specifically the Army Aviation Systems Command, just wanted to fulfill its 8(a) program obligation to give business to minorities, not thinking that the services provided would be of a quality to use. But when supplies of Bell-overhauled hubs ran low the ASI hubs were called to duty. I was told by several officials that if the men in the field had a choice, they opted for the ASI-marked equipment.

Aero Services' military contracts kept the company operating when Wichita's general aviation economy would not have been able to support it. As the war came to a close in 1975, Aero Services faced losing its contracts, though this was due more to being double-crossed than from lack of work. The government decided to give its helicopter rotor hub contract back to Bell, even though Aero Services' overhauling was of higher quality and lower price. Additionally, a new minority business surfaced to bid against me on the courier service contract, which I had previously been able to negotiate as the sole minority contractor available. This other minority contractor under-bid me at an amount that would have precluded making any profit. Months after it won the contract over me, this provider renegotiated for an amount higher than I had originally bid. I later learned that this contractor was a partnership between a Hispanic man and a white-owned company that later bought him out.

Rapidly declining income and the inability to decrease expenditures quickly enough led me to reduce personnel and sell the company's surplus aircraft to keep the business' overhead low. From our peak of about a hundred employees, we dwindled to less than ten. I had to scramble to try to regenerate my general aviation business to the extent that I had in the first part of the company's existence.

The final blow came in early 1976 when Rawdon Field owner Herb Rawdon died just prior to renegotiating Aero Services' lease agreement. If we had decided on new terms that addressed the sag in business, I might have been able to resuscitate the company. As it was, Herb's brother and business partner, Gene, had moved to California and Herb's son had long urged his father to sell the property, and sell was the first thing the younger Rawdon did following Herb's death. The land was bought by a prominent dentist and his wife, both aviation enthusiasts, who made a killing by selling the land to Beechcraft several years later when the company wanted to expand its runway across Central Avenue. Central has since changed course slightly, and Rawdon Field and its surviving buildings have been absorbed into the Beech airfield.

Over the two months after I closed out Aero Services, I moved equipment to a warehouse and put the leftover planes in storage. My indebtedness to the bank and Aero Services shareholder Roy Holloway amounted to thousands of dollars. Eventually, the fleet of courier planes was sold, as was as much rotor hub equipment as possible, mostly for scrap.

The sixteen years I spent building Aero Services constituted the most exciting period of my life. Somehow I had to decide to accept that it was over, which wasn't easy. There were many happy days I will always remember and days of sorrow I have tried to forget, but moving on was the only step that I could take. It was a step that would take me months.

—Reflections—

Augusta and I in the 1980s.

U.L. 'Rip' Gooch
The most often asked for salesman at Robinson-Lesline Buick, Inc.
Did you ask for 'Rip' when you bought your car?
Will you please ask for me the next time?

Chapter 28
A Full Plate

In the aftermath of Aero Services' closure, when I wasn't trying to find places to unload leftover equipment and materials, I worked part time doing public relations and marketing for the University Bank and continued performing pilot examinations for the FAA.

It took several months to liquidate as many assets as I could to pay the debt Aero Services incurred in its slide downward, but I was still left with a sizeable liability to the banks that financed my operation as well as the Internal Revenue Service. The banks were quite friendly in trying to work out an agreement with me; the federal tax people were quite nasty, particularly when the tax situation was built on a corporation and they decided to hold me personally liable.

Though encouraged by several people to declare bankruptcy, I did all I could not to, to keep my self-respect as well as the respect of others.

All I had left monetarily was my stake in the University Bank, which was operating well at this time. I thought that building my bank investment would be my salvation, but that would take time and I needed to find a way to keep paying my debts while helping Augusta support our family. I spent time figuring out what I should do.

I decided I had to build on the two abilities I had: as an aviator and as a salesman. Prior to leaving Rawdon Field I had applied for a position at Beechcraft, across the street. I specified a preference for sales or marketing, but also noted that any job would do. Months later, deeper in my funk, I still hadn't heard anything about an interview.

Knowing aviation opportunities were so limited, particularly for a minority person, I sought other options. My thoughts settled on automobile sales. I had never been particularly interested in automobiles, but maybe I could learn what I needed to know to sell them. No new-car dealerships in town had any black sales people. I felt that I was thinking about something that was going to cause me to break another barrier.

I started to figure out which agency I could move in on. I considered the kind of car being sold. Looking around my community I saw a number of Chevrolets and Buicks, then tried to think if I had connections to any people involved with those dealerships. Chevy dealer Don Hattan was a pilot and owned a plane and I knew his sons, who were running the business. Then

I thought of Walt Lesline, who bought an airplane from me and took lessons from Aero Services and was part owner in a Buick agency.

I filled out applications for both businesses, first going to Hattan then to Robinson-Lesline Buick. I was somewhat skeptical about either hiring me. The thing that led me to think something would come about was that I continuously saw ads looking for salesmen at both businesses. I thought I'd at least get an interview.

After Walt decided he would give me an interview, his partner, Ben Robinson, balked. Walt convinced him to let me take a psychological test to see how I would fit into the business. The test results, which were withheld from me, indicated that I would not make a good car salesman. I stopped by the dealership several times in the days following to inquire. Walt seemed to be hesitant at first to say exactly what my status was, but he did hire me in November 1976. He later said that he did so against the test results and against his partner's judgment because he thought that if I was as persistent as I appeared then I would eventually sell something. Within a year my customer list was longer than all but one of the salesmen at the dealership. In building a customer base, I started a list of people I knew from my previous business ventures and made phone calls and talked to acquaintances when I'd see them. Frequently, people coming into the dealership who happened to know me said, "Well, if you're selling cars, we want to buy one from you." With these contacts, I moved into often being the dealership's salesman of the month.

After I had worked there for awhile, Ben Robinson came by and said surprisedly, "Young man, you're going to be a successful car salesman. You can even sell cars to white folks!" Apparently, he had thought that I was brought on to sell cars to only black folks. He couldn't understand how I could come up with enough customers to allow me to stick around.

Henry Wilderom, the top salesman, who worked there for a number of years before I started, told me early on he was going to retire in the next year. He had developed many relationships in the community and he said he was going to pass on to me quite a few of his customers. However, he was so competitive that when I made more sales than he did, he got upset enough to not give me anything; he even postponed his retirement. "I don't like being beat out," Henry told me. He eventually did retire and gave his list to someone else.

When my number of car sales at Robinson-Lesline Buick passed 900 in early 1984, I decided to initiate a promotion to spur my sales, independent of the dealership. I paid for a newspaper advertisement to publicize that the driver to whom I made my 1,000th car sale would be awarded a $500 savings bond. During the 1980s, $500 could account for about five to ten percent of a new car's price, and many customers were attracted by the deal.

As a car salesman approaching my 1,000th sale, I decided to start a promotion to spur my productivity: a $500 savings bond to the customer who bought the 1,000th car.

Reaching 1,000 sales is a landmark for many car salesmen. During my time at Robinson-Lesline, 1976-93, some salesmen stayed for a week or a month, but often less than a year. Anyone who stayed around a year or two, or even four or five, often placed second to me in sales. During my promotion, someone may have come to Robinson-Lesline determined to buy a car, but they'd often ask to buy from me rather than one of the other salesmen. My sales increased significantly; people wanted to see if they'd be my 1,000 customer. Finally, I made my 1,000th sale to Lindy and Naomi Clough of Wichita.

When I first went to work with Walt's Buick dealership, he was in a period when he didn't own an airplane. I knew Walt had always liked flying. He often spoke of how when he served in the military during the 1950s, he bought an aircraft while stationed in Florida, and later he and some friends bought a plane from Aero Services. Since that time he had dropped his pilot's license due to health issues with diabetes. On several occasions while working at the dealership, I invited Walt to go flying with me because I knew how much he missed it. On a weekend when his wife was out of town and he had no plans, Walt accepted my offer. As a licensed instructor, I could allow Walt to pilot as a student, and he enjoyed the experience immensely. His interest in aviation had been rekindled, sort of like an alcoholic who's been off the sauce for a while but falls back into the habit. I took to encouraging Walt to exercise and diet so he could get his medical clearance to fly.

Soon after our flight, one of the partners in a Mooney I co-owned with a few people said he was moving away and wanted to sell his interest in the plane. I alerted Walt to the opportunity, and he decided to buy into the aircraft with the understanding that I would fly with him. In addition, when Walt's salesmen needed to go somewhere, I would fly them, thus making me both a company pilot and a car salesman. I was paid for both.

Eventually, around 1985, Walt reached the point of wanting to upgrade to a newer aircraft, and he asked me to look at the possibility of a purchasing a slightly used Beechcraft. A friend, Larry Niebler, owned one that he'd flown for several years, and offered to sell it to us. Walt considered buying it but said, "Rip, before we buy that used plane, why don't you see what it'd cost to buy a new one?" Confronted with the information I gathered, we decided to buy a new plane. Our decision came near the end of the year and there was a question of whether to buy a new airplane that was available or order the next year's model. We decided to buy the new model so we could get it decked out the way we wanted it. A perk of buying the new model was that we were able to see the plane being built in the Wichita Beech plant.

As production of the plane progressed, Walt and I also had to decide whether we wanted oxygen or air conditioning installed in the plane. The manufacture design of the aircraft prevented space for both.

I said, "I've made a lot of decisions on this thing, but I don't want to make that one. You decide."

"I know I want that oxygen, but I don't know about that air conditioning," Walt said.

To weigh our options, we took a flight in an air-conditioned model during the last weekend in August. We went up to an altitude that was cool and went to Hutchinson for lunch, after which we decided to fly some low altitude. We came into the airport to land and Walt said, "I don't have any trouble deciding what I want - I want air conditioning in that airplane!"

We knew we could use portable oxygen tanks and they'd last as long as we wanted to stay up. When we went to California, for instance, we always used the oxygen because of going over mountains. If there was bad weather and we wanted to stay above it, we also sometimes used oxygen.

Due to Walt's medical condition, everywhere he had to go I had to go and any trip we made was in the plane. Trips were taken primarily to car auctions around the country. On occasions when his wife traveled with us, he would have me bring Augusta, if it was a venture we thought she'd be interested in.

Walt and I became very close because we did so much traveling. Walt would pay me for flying, but he would often pilot the aircraft because he liked doing it so much. It counted as lessons for him because I was an instructor. We had a number of memorable experiences. En route to California, during a fuel stop in the Nevada town of Pahrump, we looked around to see a number of nice airplanes, which looked out of place there. The watering hole turned out to be the headquarters of the Chicken Ranch brothel. Walt said to someone, "Awful lot of nice planes based here." The person replied, "No, they ain't all based here; they just sort of come and go."

Another time, in the late 1980s, we stopped for fuel at Moton Field outside Tuskegee and I introduced Walt to C. Alfred "Chief" Anderson, one of the foremost leaders in black aviation and the man who had given me my first ride in an airplane decades earlier and was still an active pilot in his eighties. Walt's knowledge of aviation history and the role played in it by "Chief" Anderson caused him to consider that meeting as a very special moment in his life. Walt couldn't have been more excited if he were meeting a former president.

After several years of Walt piloting with me he accumulated a lot of experience. He did the pre-flight prep for the plane, and filed and followed the flight plan. He was so interested in everything that he asked his doctor if there was any way he could get his medical clearance. His doctor said that with exercise and a proper diet, he could get in shape to pass a flight physical. Being the committed person Walt was, he did just that. His doctor told me that motivating Walt to fly again probably added years to his life.

I helped encourage Walt Lesline, my friend and the car dealer I worked for, to fight his diabetes and regain medical clearance so he could resume flying. Walt's doctor said years were added to his life.

Walt's enthusiasm for flying was passed on to his employees, too; he eventually bought a second company plane for them to learn in and use for travel.

Chapter 29
Councilman Gooch

Since the time I arrived in Wichita, I made an effort to be a political observer. Gertrude Johnson, my initial benefactor in the city, would often take me to meetings she attended, and then when I started operating my own aviation business I started transporting or giving lessons to the individuals who were influencing life in Wichita – city officials, police, business people, lawyers and doctors.

But I never harbored a desire to be an elected official, nor to be appointed to any official capacity. That started to change in the 1970s when I was persuaded to join the Kansas Civil Rights Commission and later the governor's aviation advisory board. By the mid-1980s, while still selling cars and flying for Walt Lesline and certifying pilots for the FAA, I decided I wanted to become involved in the Wichita Airport Authority, which at the time ran the city's Mid-Continent Airport and Jabara Airport (formerly Ken-Mar). Having decades of experience and knowledge, I wanted to contribute my skills to helping make decisions about aviation in the region.

To be appointed, I would have to be nominated by a city council member and then be approved by the council. As early as when I still owned Aero Services, I approached various council members to seek a nomination. The answer I received was always no. The officials told me they knew I was well qualified and would do the job well, but they had already received requests for nominations from people who had helped them be elected to their council positions.

Even Gary Bell, the second African-American on the council, whom I had supported in his 1984 election bid, told me he had promised his Wichita Airport Authority nomination to someone else, but he would ask if that person would forego the commitment. That someone ended up being business-man Milton Glickman, father of Dan Glickman, a congressman who would later become secretary of agriculture, and Milton did not want to forfeit a chance to be on the airport board.

Two years later, in 1986, Gary Bell's council seat was being fought for by Republican Sally Dewey and Democrat Othello Curry, a longtime friend and business partner of mine. Othello would have appointed me to the Wichita Airport Authority had he won, but Ms. Dewey defeated him. As a last resort, I called Sally to ask whether she had considered whom she would appoint to the airport board, and was told to send my resume to her. She soon called me back to tell me I was the most qualified person who applied for the position, and she would be glad to nominate me for council approval for a four-year term. The Wichita City Council named me to the airport authority, and over the two years I served on it I contributed to the authority's remodeling of the Mid-Continent Airport terminal building and adding facilities to accommodate air freight planes.

At the end of those two years, the circumstances under which I had to vacate my hard-fought post would serve to illustrate just how ironic life can be.

Getting a black elected to the Wichita city council had been nearly impossible. With the exception of Gary Bell in 1985 and A. Price Woodard in the 1960s, there were none who ever made it. Part of this was due to the way elections were held. For many years the city at large would vote for council members, and the seven candidates with the most votes were appointed to two-year terms. The result was that the minority areas of Wichita were rarely represented. The black community started fighting the status quo in the 1980s, and by the time of the 1989 council election, the city assented to change the system so that the council members were elected from districts within the city and the terms were extended to four years.

The district encompassing northeast Wichita was predominantly black and democrat, but it was represented on the council by a white Republican, Sally Dewey, who had a large amount of support in the city and whose husband was a judge. Sally was a good person, a competent council member and hard worker when it came to representing our district, however, some of us felt that diversity should be represented on the council. Just the mere presence of a minority would cause issues to be raised that would otherwise be ignored. Our group of community members had previously supported Othello Curry unsuccessfully in 1986 and Gary Bell successfully in 1984. Bell, a young, likable family man, could have won in 1986 had he sought a second term, but he chose not to because he needed to support his family. Though being on the city council now pays enough to live on, the old salary did not and the job and its responsibilities took too much time for most council members to also focus on their own previous full-time occupations.

If Bell could be convinced to run in the 1989 election, the black community thought there was a good chance to achieve some diversity again. Gary first agreed to pursue the position but had to withdraw because he decided to accept a new job that required him to move from Wichita. Though disappointed, we realized he had to take the opportunity. Our secondary choice was a professor at Wichita State University, Dr. John Gaston. Convincing him was difficult. As the deadline to file candidacy for the primary approached, Dr. Gaston waffled.

I finally received a phone call from Othello Curry telling me that John Gaston had just said definitively that he would not run because his university workload was too heavy. "We need to get your name on the ballot, Rip," Othello said. That came as a surprise to me. I had no desire to run because I knew how being on the council would affect my ability to support my family. Additionally, I couldn't believe anyone would think I would be qualified. I called John to verify that he wasn't going to run. The filing deadline for the primary was several days away. Gary Bell had previously also mentioned my name as a possible candidate, telling me, "Of all the candidates talked about, believe it or not, your name comes up quite often."

Temporarily homebound from a light hernia operation, I called some people in the community for an evening meeting at my house to finalize a united course of action. The eight of us discussed the situation from all sides, with Augusta repeatedly saying no to all suggestions that I run. Then Jo Brown, the wife of my physician, said, "Rip, this community needs you in office." The word "need" swayed me to think I should try for office; until that time people kept saying they "wanted" me to run, which is a significant difference.

Someone noted that there would be times when I would have to make impromptu speeches at various functions, and suggested I give a sample speech. Thinking of that later made me wonder if the person had noticed my slight speech impediment, which I usually am able to mask by choosing words carefully and not speaking fast. It brought to mind a statement Gertrude Johnson made to me some years before, that if I didn't have a speaking problem, she'd want to back me for elected office. My following acceptance speech, though, didn't seem to turn anyone off.

"There won't be any more talk," Jo Brown said. "You are going to the courthouse tomorrow to file. We are going to settle who is running." I asked her about my hernia, and how her husband, Val, had said, "Don't even lift anything as heavy as a night gown." She countered that Val would make sure a wheelchair would be provided to me.

At the filing deadline, I found out that John Gaston had also filed to run despite his statements otherwise; some of his students had convinced him to do so. At a candidate meeting soon after, I looked him in the eye and told him what I thought, finishing with the promise that I would kick his ass in the election. After some words, we agreed that the issue was to have minority representation on the council and the loser of the primary would support the winner in the final election.

Additionally, I made sure to visit Sally Dewey in person to tell her I would be running for the office, not against her. I told her that those of us in the black community appreciated how she represented the district, but that we felt a person of color should be on the council. Sally, who gained my respect when she had appointed me to the Wichita Airport Authority, told me that if she had to lose she couldn't think of anyone she would feel better losing to. We agreed to run a clean race.

I started attending council meetings on a regular basis and planning my strategy. Observing how campaigns were run on the state level, I decided to open a full-time campaign headquarters, which had never been done for a Wichita city council election. At Jo Brown's recommendation, I named as my campaign manager a local minister named Titus James. He was young, aggressive and rapidly gaining recognition in the community; he attended meetings and other activities I could not. The fact that he headed a congregation and appealed to young voters also helped the campaign. Calling many of the people I knew well in addition to those who had done business with me through Robinson-Lesline Buick and Aero Services, I secured enough monetary contributions to run what I thought could be an effective campaign. Many donors came from outside my district, and it is likely that more were Republican than Democrat, due to lack of partisanship in city council elections.

I recruited 12 volunteers to work in different areas of the district and asked those 12 key people to bring on 12 more people, who got 12 more full-time supporters to help with the campaign, the strategy being to involve as many people as possible. They fanned out to deliver pamphlets and promote me. The effort paid off; I was one of the two candidates to advance to the general election; Sally Dewey was the other. John Gaston stopped by my headquarters to shake my hand and offer his support to me in my efforts. He apologized for his college supporters not following his lead, but promised he'd try to win them over to my side. The next battle would be the final push for a council seat.

A phone bank was installed in campaign headquarters for volunteers to call voters. Days before the election I contracted to have an airplane tow a banner over the city, reading "Vote Rip Gooch for City Council." People who knew me from my aviation work often thought I piloted the plane, which I never denied. My treasurer, Dr. William Burney Sr., worried about the expenditures, but I told him I wouldn't hold him responsible; as it happened, my campaign was never late paying any bills. We finished with a large advertising budget and funds left over. The strategic campaigning was so different and attention-catching for that time in local politics that I don't think most people expected it. It broadened my recognition and developed into water-cooler conversation at local workplaces.

"You're up against an incumbent and that's a real challenge," I recall thinking. "Being up against a white female incumbent is like fighting a mountain." Even my wife, Augusta, thought I wouldn't be elected because my reputation had largely been associated with aviation, and the public at large didn't know me, but she supported me and I don't think anyone worked harder on the campaign. I went into election night in November 1989 without a clue as to the outcome. I intentionally stayed away from my headquarters, instead going to the county office building where the news media watched the precinct-by-precinct counts. When I returned to headquarters, all were concerned as to where I'd been. I don't know how I would have adjusted myself to show up as a loser, but when I walked in with the most up-to-date information, I felt very secure in facing my people and thanking the many who made the likely success possible. The official announcement of my victory was made shortly after my arrival.

Becoming the third black to win a seat on the Wichita City Council prompted local media to swarm me on election night 1989.

News people trickled in and stuck microphone after microphone in my face as they asked, "How do you feel about the race and the challenge ahead?" I was excited, but I knew I had been elected to serve and would serve to the best of my ability. With cameras rolling and lights flashing, I suddenly felt I'd been put in a position to accomplish something, but really didn't think I was prepared to do the job expected of me. However, the confidence held in me by the voters boosted my resolve.

After I was sworn into the Wichita, Kansas, city council in 1989, a friend told me he had never seen someone raise their hand so high. My wife Augusta stood by my side.

Soon after the final numbers were announced, I received a call from Sally Dewey expressing her congratulations. My success can be credited to the broad support across racial and political lines. The people of north Wichita wanted and needed a winner then, and they got it. The swearing in ceremony was one of the proudest moments of my life. Augusta stood beside me as I took my oath. Gene Jackson, one of the twin brother owners of Jackson Mortuary, said, "Rip, I never saw anybody who, when they said, 'Raise your hand to swear in,' raised their hand so high. You had your hand and arm all the way up when you said, 'I do solemnly swear.'" After the swearing in, I'd never had so many hands to shake. Once I was allowed to sit in my council meeting chair for the first time, I was sure I had become a part of the political system.

Though there were nights when I would wake up thinking, "Where am I?" and "What am I supposed to do?" I was never truly afraid because my associates and community advocates offered strong support. Additionally, I had learned much from the council meetings I had watched since announcing my candidacy. The job as a city council member isn't always a popular one, but being in city government is challenging and exciting. Much is said about how much people complain to elected officials, but the officials are basically elected to listen to complaints. Serving on the city council proved particularly challenging because I wanted to see changes and improvements as immediately as possible. My motto has always been, "Gaining for yourself so that you may be able to give to others." Now that I had a position on the council, I intended to give minorities in Wichita the representation we had often been denied. Reality set in as I grew tired and perturbed at hearing the repeated phrase, "Let's do a study," concerning every issue presented to the council before almost any action could be taken. Ironically, my first recommendation to the council was to perform a study concerning improvements in northeast Wichita, which encompassed the black, Hispanic and Asian areas of the city. The area had many rundown buildings that were housing indigents and drug addicts as well as small businesses that were not bringing much benefit to the area. Though it was a part of the city that desperately needed revitalization, it was also the type of area that could easily be neglected for years to come because most council members had no association with it and would also avoid traveling through it because they thought it was dangerous.

To convince the council to take action I knew a focus had to be put on the part of the area that could garner the most attention, Wichita State University, which sat on the east edge of the redevelopment area. Many Wichitans had attended WSU and cheered its athletic teams, and by promoting the redevelopment area as the city's gateway to the university, we gained enough community support to start work.

The tasks included fixing or removing the dilapidated structures in the neighborhood, such as a half-empty apartment building that housed a number of vagrants and drug addicts and was located near a city park that had fallen into disuse for obvious reasons. Some in the area opposed what they considered the ruining of their neighborhood, and one business posted a sign reading, "Impeach Rip Gooch." The few small businesses there thought they were being wronged, but their lack of growth potential and productivity outweighed their arguments. Though even now the redevelopment has not been completed, new businesses have moved in, part of 21st Street (the main artery through the area) has been widened, and many residential neighborhoods have been cleaned up. Once the ball started moving, people decided to roll with it, and now many residents voice satisfaction with the improvements that have been made in the past fifteen years. Now the major complaint is that the city is taking too long to complete the project.

A main factor in the revitalization of northeast Wichita was safety. I lobbied for a police substation in this part of the city, an idea opposed by a majority of the council. The city manager agreed to look into the feasibility of the idea, though. At the same time leaders of a 21st Street church approached the council to complain that the widening of the road had resulted in their building's entrance being dangerously close to traffic; the church leaders requested the city purchase their building for demolition or other use. During the council meeting in which both substation approval and the church purchase were up for vote, discussion on the issues was deadlocked. To obtain a vote – and appease the church congregation, whose opinion I supported – the city manager suggested to the council that the church could be purchased, the back part of it could be used as a police substation and the street-side half could be torn down. The issue passed, but nothing was done to convert the church. Existence of a police substation seemed promising at that time, but it did not actually happen until a few years after I left office, by which point substations in at least one part of the city were already built.

Another controversial issue I fought for while on the city council included a stoplight at the busy intersection of 13th and Hydraulic streets. A number of elderly people and children lived in the neighborhood and had to take their lives in their hands when they crossed the intersection. After a community member presented the problem to me, I requested information on the issue from the traffic department and was told the intersection was too close to another traffic light to have a light of its own. After finding other intersections in the city with two traffic lights within a similar distance, I insisted the traffic department's objection was groundless, and a light was installed.

When a community learning center operated by the Urban League on a corner plagued by drug dealers sought to expand, I approached the head of a savings and loan company that held the mortgage on an adjoining lot. He was someone I'd come to know through serving on a committee for the Kansas Aviation Museum, and over lunch we discussed how his company could probably gain more out of the land by donating it and counting it as a tax credit than by selling it, if it could find anyone to buy it. After he read some material about what the Urban League and the learning center did, he agreed to donate the property.

Also during my time on the council, groundwork was set for construction of a nature trail and center in the north part of my district. Then U.S. Sen. Bob Dole offered federal funds to the project if state money was also pledged. The Great Plains Nature Center now covers nearly 300 acres and is home to 125 species of wildflowers and 160 types of birds, among other animals.

Less than a year through my city council term, in September 1990, Augusta and I suffered a tremendous emotional blow. Our son, Kerry, had been working for slightly more than a year at Beech Aircraft in a marketing job that, among other things, required him to pilot planes to customers and dealers around the country. He was the first black to have a flying job with Beech and showed enough potential that the company, in an effort to strengthen his abilities for possible promotion into management, loaned him to the charitable organization United Way. Companies that contribute to United Way often loan select employees to the organization for weeks or months at a time to help raise funds. One day during the time he was training for United Way, Kerry stopped by his office at Beech to visit with co-workers and was approached by an associate named Chuck about taking a flight the following day - September 12 - to Conway, Arkansas, to take a visiting friend home. The flight would allow them to contribute flight hours to their company proficiency requirements, which would help Kerry because he would not be flying for Beech during the period of his loan to United Way. It was decided Chuck would pilot to Arkansas and Kerry would pilot for the return trip. On arrival at the small Conway airport, Chuck misjudged the landing and crashed the Beech Baron 58 at the end of the runway and into a house, causing a fire. Chuck's friend and another passenger exited at the back of the plane, but Kerry and Chuck were trapped in front.

Augusta and I heard and saw news reports about an accident involving a Beech-owned plane, and we told each other we were glad Kerry was still in training with United Way and not in the air. I tried to contact Kerry on his mobile phone, but was unsuccessful. Out of sight of Augusta, so as to not worry her, I continued to try to call Kerry every half-hour or so. The last news reports we heard that evening said one pilot had been killed and one seriously injured. When a car pulled into our driveway at about midnight, and two men got out, I met them at the front door and immediately asked them whether Kerry was the injured one or the one who didn't make it. Kerry was killed on impact, said the men, who were from Beech. Chuck suffered major burns and later died at hospital.

Kerry was 25 years old. Flying was his love, and Augusta and I both knew it and shared it with him. Losing him hurt us more than anything we'd ever experienced. I find it very hard to explain the real effect his death had on my life; the only people who could understand this are those who have lost children to death. Augusta and I received some solace in talking with one of the crash survivors who said that Kerry had tried to tell Chuck the landing wouldn't work, indicating that Kerry's previous experience as a flight instructor allowed him to accurately judge the situation. Augusta and I knew at that point that the crash would not have happened if Kerry had been piloting.

My son Kerry's flight-instructing experience could have saved his life. Here, he shakes the hand of his first student to qualify for a private license while I beam with pride in front of the Cessna 172 his mother and I bought him.

Some people say good things can come from tragedy. That did turn out to be the case as far as Kerry was concerned. A conversation between Wichita Mayor Bob Knight and an executive at Coastal Oil (whose identity I don't know) resulted in the oil executive deciding to establish a four-year college scholarship in memory of Kerry to be available to the children of city employees who attend Wichita State University. The executive was a WSU alumnus and I worked for the city, thus his choice of requirements. The responses and communication I have had from several students who received scholarships have told me how much the awards helped them with their accomplishments in life. That in itself has had a great healing effect for me. Of great consolation also was the birth of Kerry's son, Kerry Jr., four months after his death. Watching Kerry Jr. grow up has helped fill the void his father left.

Prior to losing Kerry, I planned to retire when my council term ended. I would be 69 years old. Though there were things I still wanted to accomplish, I had felt I would be able to pass the baton to Kerry and let him succeed while I derived fulfillment from witnessing him do that. With his death and the frustration I often experienced at not being able to fully serve the community through the city council, I decided retirement was not an option. The city council's members had elected me for a one-year term as vice mayor during my third year there, and that helped me realize that I might stand a chance to move higher on the political ladder and made me feel that accomplishing governmental tasks could be enjoyable. To boost relations with Wichita's sister city, the council sent me to Orleans, France, where Augusta and I were treated as royalty (complete with a chauffeured car). Perhaps the most thrilling experience of my council years came when the Kansas

During a city council goodwill trip to Wichita's sister city, Orleans, France, Augusta and I visited Paris.

Guard invited me to fly a Phantom F-4 jet, a unique experience for me because I had never been in such an aircraft.

Such new perks did not lull me into contentment. Thinking that if I were to reach the Kansas Legislature I could better serve my constituency, I started planning to take the next step in my life.

I was thrilled when the Kansas Guard invited me to fly a Phantom F-4 jet during my council years.

Chapter 30
Senator Gooch

My campaign for state Senate in 1992 was different than my previous city ones. To start with, I was running in a recently redistricted area that had no incumbent. Additionally, I had name recognition and more experience than the other candidates. I kept my previous campaign manager but I changed treasurer, replaced other team members, and picked up some strong, hardworking individuals. I easily won the election held in November. I resigned from the city council at the end of the year, a few months before the end of my four-year term.

My tour of duty in the state capitol in Topeka would end up lasting eleven years. I served under three governors – Democrat Joan Finney for two years, Republican Bill Graves for eight, and Democrat Kathleen Sebelius for two.

Until the 1992 election there had been only four other African-Americans to serve full Senate terms in the more-than-100-year history of the Kansas Legislature: George Haley from Kansas City; and Curtis McClinton, Billy McCray and Eugene Anderson from Wichita. McClinton and Haley served at the same time, and ever since have kidded each other as to who was sworn in first.

Anticipating my duties in the Senate would take up more time than my city duties, I resigned most of my other responsibilities. For a part-time paying position in the Kansas Senate I gave up three income-producing jobs: selling cars and flying for the Buick agency, and being an FAA pilot examiner, a position I maintained for 28 years. The

George Haley, former Kansas state senator and ambassador to Gambia, greets my grandchildren and me in the Kansas Senate chamber in 2000. Haley, his brother Alex (author of *Roots*) and I once played together in the streets of Henning, Tennessee.

situation held a certain amount of irony because for more than forty years, aviation had served to consistently elevate my station in life. Now, I had reached a point that required me to leave the profession that had taken me worlds away from the cotton fields of Tennessee. Because of my love for aviation and long experience, I continued to fly for personal convenience and enjoyment, even introducing it to my grandson.

Being sworn into the Kansas Senate in January 1993 was similar to my entry onto the Wichita City Council. Even though Augusta wasn't able to stand beside me, she was in the chamber to wish me well. Because serving at the state capitol required me to spend weekdays in Topeka, Augusta decided to retire from teaching so she could join me for the four months or so a year that the Legislature met. Our weekends were spent back in Wichita

Following the Kansas Senate's oath of office ceremony, Augusta joined me at my new desk.

My journey in state government started out very positively. I was fortunate to enter my position and have a secretary who had worked for two other senators, Velda Duette. First she worked for Eugene Anderson and followed with Jim Ward, whom I succeeded in the 29th district when redistricting placed his residence outside the district's boundaries. Being black, Velda was familiar with the issues I was specifically interested in

Velda Duette, my first Senate secretary, showed me the ropes.

and understood some of the circumstances I'd face. During her time working for me, she was also elected vice chair of the Kansas Democratic Party, so she served as an even greater asset through her connections. Freshmen senators are assigned to work closely with veteran senators to learn the ropes, but I received more education on the workings of the Legislature from Velda. She served as my right and left hands for eight years, until she died unexpectedly. Even though I thought replacing Velda would be difficult, Carolyn Wims-Campbell, who had previous experience working for another senator, did an excellent job. Carolyn always credits Velda with training her.

During my time in the Legislature, Velda was the only African-American secretary among those serving the senators and Senate leadership. The lack of African-Americans among the more than 100 non-custodial employees at the capitol was an issue I raised consistently during my Senate years. At that time there were five African-Americans employed in the capitol building, excluding janitorial staff. According to my most recent count, that number has increased by one.

One way I could somewhat shift the balance on my own was through engaging young African-Americans to serve as interns and

Carolyn Wims-Campbell was my second Senate secretary.

Senate pages as often as possible. Interns usually come from colleges around the state, such as Washburn University in Topeka and the University of Kansas in nearby Lawrence. One exceptional intern I had was Janet Lewis of Wichita, a particularly attentive, hardworking and impressive young woman. She has progressed to become a successful attorney.

Pages, who work one day at the capitol as errand runners for the legislators, come from middle schools and high schools across the state. Though legislators are required to find pages, many call us to volunteer.

To achieve more diversity, I made direct contact with churches and social organizations to locate youths who often knew nothing about the opportunity to serve as pages. The duties of pages range from delivering important papers to legislators to fetching a Coke for a weary senator who has spent hours in the Senate chambers listening to legislation. The experience allows pages to observe the legislative process firsthand. At the end of the day, the pages receive a nominal check and a photo of themselves with the legislator who invited them to serve and the governor. In my Senate office I displayed copies of the photos in poster frames on a wall. While I was in office, some of the pages grew old enough to vote for me. In some cases I've been able to keep track of their progress in life.

I've kept photos of all the pages who served me in the Kansas Senate. This typical one shows Gov. Kathleen Sebelius with, from right, William Roberson, Jonathan Batts and Marissa Batts in February 2003.

Due to my political affiliation and my skin color, I was in two minority groups in the Senate. There were only 16 Democrats among the 40 newly elected senators, and for eight years, Sherman Jones from Kansas City and I were the only two blacks. One of the first orders of business at the beginning of the senators' four-year terms is for each party to elect their respective leaders. The leaders then select who serves on what committees

For several years Sherman Jones of Kansas City was the only black in the Kansas Senate besides me.

and what issues the Senate hears. At the beginning of my first term, I did not realize that many people lobby for leadership and committee positions far in advance. Sherman Jones, who had previously served in the Kansas House of Representatives, offered me some pointers. One thing he noted was that, judging by the makeup of the Democratic membership, he and I would probably be the deciding votes in the selection of the minority leader from among the three people pursuing the position. He suggested we leverage the opportunity, by making requests for the office and committee assignments we desired. We received everything we wanted.

The minority leader we elected, Jerry Carr, had been in office two terms prior to my election, and was a likable and knowledgeable person. Though he didn't appear to be a fighter for issues, he would negotiate solutions and not bend to pressure from the opposing side. After four years of Carr's leadership, the Democrats elected Anthony Hensley, who served throughout my last two terms in office. He was quite sharp and was more of a hardball player than a negotiator.

Because of my city council experience, I decided I could be most effective working on committees that would address issues concerning city government. During the eleven years I served in the Senate, my committee assignments included: Ranking Minority Member of both the Committee on Federal and State Affairs and the Committee on Transportation; Member of the Committee on Elections and Local Government, Joint Committee on Administrative Rules and Regulations, and the Joint Committee on Economic Development.

Bills on the Senate docket arrive there only after receiving approval from committees. Bills can deal with issues as vast as funding for education and highways to small items such as naming a state amphibian. When issues emerged that would affect minorities, I naturally took interest in them, but I did not limit my scope. I took a broad range of experience to the Senate, including years as a taxpayer, city councilman, business owner, union member, aviator, banker laborer, husband, father, and underprivileged child, and I aimed to support measures that I felt would be the best course of action for everybody involved.

One of the first issues I advocated heavily happened to focus on a minority-related bill, which would have established the African-American Affairs Commission, a group that would investigate issues affecting blacks and work to make those issues known to legislators. The bill had been proposed before I was elected, but had not progressed, though there existed a Hispanic Affairs Commission. With a Democratic governor, Joan Finney, in office when I entered the Senate, I assumed action could be quickly taken toward advancing the program, but I was wrong. Getting this program proposal out of committee was my first major political lesson in how the legislature works. After trying for some time to win committee approval for the bill, I finally convinced the committee chair to give the bill a hearing. Prior to the meeting, I requested that supporters of the commission come and speak to the committee and I made sure the presenters were prepared and understood how long to speak, etc., so the committee could vote during the hour that was allotted to each hearing. The plan went awry when an additional person, a minister who did not know the plan of action, insisted on making a statement and used nearly all the time that was allowed for the meeting. With minutes to spare, the chair asked if anyone else cared to speak (in which case the hearing could be continued at a later time), but no one did. I immediately made a motion to vote to move the bill to the floor of the Senate. The committee chairman, who had been instructed to do what he could to not let the issue out of committee, rapped the gavel and said time had expired, paying no heed to the senator who seconded my motion. Though the chairman could have brought the subject up at a later committee hearing, he never did.

Upset, I spent some time researching other ways the bill could reach the floor for discussion. I found I could request that it be withdrawn from the committee and brought to the floor for a vote on whether to discuss the issue. A senior senator advised me to use this as a last resort because it was not very well accepted to bypass a committee chair and required approval of two-thirds of the forty senators to pass. Though Sherman Jones joined me in speaking on the floor to encourage support, we fell short, with only 17 people in favor of discussion - 16 Democrats and one Republican. This was one of my major disappointments in the Senate. It also served to brand me as a "bad boy" in the Legislature for having maneuvered around my committee chairman and the instructions he'd received. In 1997, the African-American Affairs Commission bill finally became law after the bill was introduced and passed in the House and brought to the Senate for a vote. The representative who originated the bill and pushed it through the house was white.

During my second term, a bill was proposed in the Senate to allow two weeks instead of one week for short-term expulsions from schools. After it appeared the bill would pass I tried to make an amendment to the bill, to require the schools to provide some kind of alternative supervised programming for the students while they were suspended. The bill passed without my amendment. During the floor fight, I asked what senators expected to happen while the kids were out of school, and bill supporters responded that the parents should take a vacation if their children were suspended from school. To me, that was a stupid idea. To them, it obviously wasn't.

Compared to city government, I found it harder at the state level to accomplish anything because of the number of people who needed to be swayed in order to make legislative changes. Highway funding always triggered approval of additional funds for multiple years, but education funding was a subject on which we could never compromise until the end of a session.

Until the last half of my second term, Augusta and I often followed a regular schedule of spending weekdays in Topeka and weekends in Wichita. She loved the role of a senator's wife, and she attended legislative wives events, as well as receptions and conventions. Though she occasionally voiced complaints about experiencing pain, it wasn't until 1996 when we found the problem. While on a trip to the Bayou Classic football game in New Orleans and the National Black Caucus of State Elected Officials in Biloxi, Mississippi, her pain became so intense that we decided to cut the trip short so she could return to Wichita to seek medical attention. Within two weeks, we found that she had multiple myeloma, a rare form of cancer that grows in bone marrow. She immediately began chemotherapy but initially felt well enough to return to Topeka with me in January. Her condition quickly deteriorated, making her unable to make the trips. I started spending as much time with her as I could, driving two hours home in the evening when my Senate work was done and driving back to Topeka the next morning. We had been together forty-nine years, and I refused to be separated from her by placing her in a care facility. Instead, I made sure she had 24-hour home care. She passed away on August 12, 1997. Losing Kerry during my council years and then Augusta affected my outlook, and I struggled physically and emotionally throughout the ordeal, but I did not let that interfere with the work that had to be done.

My wife Augusta and I were months short of being married 49 years when she died of cancer in 1997, in the middle of my tenure in the Kansas Senate.

Some of my pain would be eased by non-Senate activities. On one occasion, the city of Salina, Kansas, requested that I speak at a ceremony honoring one of its former mayors, Charles Caldwell. I was deeply moved by the opportunity because Charles had been a close friend, supported my political campaigns and also led a life that closely paralleled mine. We each had two beautiful daughters and a younger son, and we met while one of his girls was competingin the Miss Black Teen Kansas pageant with my daughter Bonita. He had been a teacher and principal, and I had been a flight teacher. He served as a city councilman and mayor, and I had been a city councilman and vice-mayor. He served in the state House of Representatives, I served in the state Senate. We shared tragedy as well. His son died in a car accident while mine died in an aircraft accident, and our wives both died of cancer. Our friendship lasted until he died a few years ago.

A few years later I received an honor of my own when I was a named a member of the inaugural class of the Black Aviation Hall of Fame, which was established in 2001 in Memphis. In conjunction with my induction, my hometown of Ripley, Tennessee, saluted me as the guest of honor at its annual Labor Day parade and presented me with a key to the city. It is among the greatest honors I have received and will forever cherish because I remember being a poor child for whom the Labor Day celebrations provided one weekend of joy and celebration in an otherwise limited existence. The experience was something I never would have envisioned while growing up. The honor was particularly special because the Labor Day

James Carthell Hayes, my best friend for seventy years, provides support at my Black Aviation Hall of Fame induction.

parade was tied to one of the few and fondest memories I have of my mother – riding with her on the back of a beautiful horse in the 1927 parade.

Commemorating my induction in the Black Aviation Hall of Fame in 2001, my hometown of Ripley, Tennessee, gave me the key to the city and asked me to lead the Labor Day parade, which rekindled memories of when my mother carried me on a horse in the parade in the mid-1920s. Here I'm joined by my cousin Albert Murray.

Though no longer flying on a professional basis, I maintained active status in various flight organizations and served as a paid marketing consultant for Raytheon Aircraft for three years in the late 1990s. The position enabled me to

During my time serving in the Kansas State Senate, I worked as a marketing consultant for Raytheon Aircraft.

socialize with a number of successful and sometimes famous individuals such as the attorneys Johnnie Cochran and Willie E. Gary, boxing promoter Don King, boxer Evander Holyfield, actor Clifton Davis and magazine publisher Earl Graves. During this time, I was also able to initiate a 1996 meeting in Wichita that led to joining the seven major black aviation associations under one umbrella as the International Black Aerospace Council. The move would make it easier for the groups to obtain corporate sponsorship for their events. The president of each of the seven organizations serves on the Council's board. The organizations are the Tuskegee Airmen Inc., Organization of Black Airline Pilots, U.S.

Marketing for Raytheon Aircraft allowed me to meet such notable people as attorney Johnnie Cochran.

Army Black Aviators, Negro Airmen International, Black Pilots of America, National Black Coalition of Federal Aviation Employees, and Bessie Coleman Foundation (named for the pioneering black aviatrix).

I initiated the meeting in Wichita that resulted in the formation of the International Black Aerospace Council.

When I could help young African-Americans further their interest in aviation, I tried. A number of times I questioned the commander of the Kansas Air National Guard as to why he had no black aircraft pilots in the state. He always said none applied. I became aware of an aviation-oriented young black graduate of the University of Kansas who had received an ROTC commission but could not fly in the Air Force because there were no flight school openings for him. There were openings in the Guard, of course, and the young man looked like a perfect fit. I arranged an interview for him with the Guard commander. The young man's name was Grant Gooch, and as we walked into the colonel's office and Grant introduced himself as a "Gooch," the colonel said, "Well, in that case, we definitely have a spot for you!" Grant and I did not know at that time that we are distant relatives. The commander made sure Grant was placed in the Guard's next available flight class. After training in the Guard for about two years, Grant flew F-16s in the Kansas Guard for only a year or so until the F-16 unit was eliminated. He transferred to Iowa to keep flying F-16s, at which point Kansas lost its only black Guard pilot.

During my final Senate years I became greatly disenchanted with the political process, which led me to think I should have remained on the

Wichita city council. The issues that emerged showed me how powerless elected officials are as they ascend to higher levels of government.

Strong arguments raged on such issues as the death penalty and prison terms. A successful bill I fought for allowed for review of cases of prisoners with terminal health conditions to consider releasing them to family members' custody. I also fought against overly harsh drug laws that convicted people to long-term sentences on small-quantity drug or paraphernalia possession charges. I feel the punishment should fit the crime and that it's ridiculous when the cost to house prisoners is several times greater than the cost to rehabilitate them. My greatest accomplishment in the Senate was pushing a

One of the two times I was asked to serve as chairman of the Senate for a day.

bill enacted in 2003 that provided drug rehabilitation as an alternative to prison for some offenders, but I was frustrated because the bill was stripped of its ability to help those who had already been convicted to long prison terms. And so, we have some people serving short terms for petty drug offenses and getting out before those already serving time for the same offenses. Offenders received an additional strike when at about the same time the state parole board, which previously had been reduced from seven members to five, was reduced to three. Just three people were responsible for the future of any person coming before them. I was very concerned that the board might be all white when 40 percent of Kansas' jail population is black.

A major hot-button issue that burned me involved racial profiling by police. Several years before my 2003 retirement, I introduced an anti-racial profiling bill. The bill was debated on the floor but could not gain enough support to pass because the senators weren't convinced there was a problem. They did agree to accept a substitute bill to finance a study that would document whether the problem existed. Several hundred thousand dollars was allotted for the study, which was completed two years before I retired. It revealed profiling did exist, but no action was taken on it until after I left the Senate. In 2005, Gov. Kathleen Sebelius signed an anti-racial profiling bill into law, under the sponsorship of the senator who replaced me, Donald Betts. By that point the bill had been watered down so much that it was almost an anti-racial profiling measure in name only.

Possibly the final incident that led me to decide to leave the Senate was the longest-running battle I've ever waged, and it continues even now, years after I've left office. It did not involve any legislative action, but was a battle for which I used all the resources and channels available to me as a state senator. A woman from my district approached me in 1999 to assist her in seeking custody of a grandson. The infant was in the foster care system, and the grandmother had repeatedly asked the Kansas Department of Social and Rehabilitation Services what she would need to do to assume custody. She fulfilled all the requirements of special training and other measures the department requested. Despite that, the SRS would not turn the child over to her, even though she could support him without government funding, which would have saved the state years of foster care expense. In the time I spent working for the grandmother's cause, I had multiple discussions with three successive governor-appointed secretaries of SRS, attempting to solicit help from them. Each admitted the case had not been properly handled, but none would override the local office's decision and award custody to the grandmother.

The child had been placed in a rural two-woman foster household. The women were white; the child was black. Eventually, the women were able to adopt him. They also held foster custody of several other children. Soon after the adoption state health officials removed these children from the residence due to sanitation problems in the house, but the child at the center of my battle could not be removed because he had been adopted. By this time SRS had paid foster care money to the women for three years; the money could have been saved had the grandmother been dealt with properly.

I started identifying more and more with the child's situation, though I have never met him. Like me, he had been a child with no permanent home, and that is a circumstance that affects me deeply. Every time I hear a song called "Stand" by Donnie McClurkin, I think about the efforts the grandmother and I had taken to help the child: "What do you do when you've done all you can and it seems like it's never enough? And what do you say when your friends turn away and you're all alone? … Well, you just stand."

The child is now placed in a questionable household for what could be the rest of his formative years. Legally, neither his grandmother nor I can follow his story. If his home life is safe and happy, good. If it's bad, that is unfortunate because he is too young to run away or realize that he can report his situation to authorities.

Will he be able to transcend his roots and find success or happiness in life? Only time can tell, but I will keep wondering.

At the close of my eleventh session in the Kansas Legislature, the entire Senate officially recognized me in Resolution 1876 for being the oldest senator and the only one to have served in World War II. Even though the recognition may not have been intentionally planned as a farewell, it turned out that way. During the summer I considered my lack of progress in fighting for a number of issues. As my 80th birthday approached that September, I grew serious about not returning.

For my birthday, I planned a celebration that could be what I would have wanted as a real going-away party from the Senate as well as a celebration of my eighty years of life. The celebration consisted of a full day of activities I enjoyed.

My 80th birthday celebration banquet was attended by several hundred guests, who were serenaded by jazz pianist and Kansas City legend Jay McShann.

Starting the morning of September 13, I held a golf tournament and invited my friends and associates from the Wichita city council, the Legislature, the aviation world, childhood friends and people who just loved to golf. I was fortunate that Lt. Gen. Daniel James, commander of the U.S. Air Guard, was in Kansas that weekend and able to attend my celebration. This was special to me because of my past association with his father "Chappie" James, the first black four-star general in the Air Force.

Even though rain interrupted completion of the tournament, the informal ceremony to award prizes turned into a lively and enjoyable event. That evening at a local hotel, a few hundred people joined me for my birthday banquet, which included a mini-roast and a musical performance by Kansas City jazz pianist Jay McShann, who had led the 1940s big band that exposed the world to saxophonist Charlie Parker. After this daylong affair, dubbed "Celebrate 80," I finalized my decision to announce my retirement from the Senate.

My 80th birthday celebration included a golf tournament attended by (far right) U.S. Air Guard Commander Daniel James, son of "Chappie," and (center) Air Guard Lt. Col. Grant Gooch, whom I helped enter the Guard.

—Reflections—

Gooch family members, young and old, reunite every few years. The infrequency of such gatherings is an obstacle many families now face in trying to pass traditions and knowledge on to younger generations.

Conclusion

After eleven sessions in the Kansas Senate, frustration building inside me, I announced my retirement on December 18, 2003, choosing that day because it was the anniversary of my proposal to my wife in 1947 and our marriage in 1948. My retirement was effective January 2, a year before my term was to have ended.

Upon retiring, I intended to add to my 20,000 hours of flight time and compile my memories in book form so my grandchildren and their offspring would be able to appreciate where they came from. It was the kind of information that I wish I had been able to more easily access. I have often wondered as my years roll by faster and faster how much our lives are dependent upon others and how short life really is. Life from the perspective of more than four score years has given me the hindsight to see that the dreams I had were really made possible by the people who believed in me and encouraged me by their example to believe in myself. It wasn't that I had never acknowledged my gratitude, but I wanted to recognize those persons whom I never had the privilege to know as well as those that I had known and whose involvement in my life – both positive and negative – had helped me grow.

That goal completed, I wanted to provide a wider audience with the inspiration that comes from learning about an underdog who succeeds and the awareness that despite how far this country has come in cultivating better race relations, we have a long way to go.

When I arrived in Wichita, Kansas, a few years prior to the U.S. Supreme Court's 1954 decision in Brown v. the Topeka Board of Education, I could not patronize the restaurants or hotels of my choice, play golf on any local courses, swim in any public pools, or choose my children's elementary school. In the five decades since, this has changed and we have experienced full integration of U.S. military forces, elected a number of minorities to both houses of Congress and seen them appointed to presidential cabinet positions. We now have African-Americans serving as presidents and athletic coaches at previously all-white colleges, and as mayors and city managers in major cities. In the world of aviation, all major airlines and many corporations now employ black pilots, and a number of prosperous African-American business owners can afford to own and operate jet aircraft.

Yet the ratio of blacks to whites in these professions is much lower than that in the general population, which is 12 percent black. Among the 117 head coaches at Division 1-A college football programs, three are African-Americans as of the 2005 school year – down from a high of eight in 1997. In the Air Force one in five members are black, but only one in twenty pilots are black. Of the 129,000 total pilots/navigators employed in this country, 0.5 percent are black, according to the U. S. Census Bureau. This means there are fewer black pilots flying professionally today than at the end of the World War II Tuskegee flight program, which produced about 1,000 graduates.

In Kansas, where I've worked to try to bring blacks into my areas of influence (aviation and politics), there remains not one black pilot in the state Air Guard or in a pilot post for any major corporation. I previously addressed how among several hundred non-custodial employees in the state capitol building, there are only six blacks.

Education and economics hold the key to bringing a realistic change to society. Here, I'm not just talking about education in our schools. I'm talking about social education that takes place when we learn to understand and tolerate our cultural commonality as well as our differences. This kind of education must take place on both sides of the fence and can better prepare all of us to be a part of a positive change in racial relations. We must eliminate prejudiced attitudes and increase acceptance and respect for one another.

Once the country begins to see how it benefits from economic inclusion by all, I believe these positive economic changes will become permanent. I like to use Atlanta as an example of an area that has thrived by encouraging economic inclusion. Once it became clear that economic opportunity existed for all, many of the country's most brilliant African-Americans started to flock to the area. With a talented and diverse pool of workers, corporations followed, infusing more money and other well-paid executives, administrators and workers into the city. Now, it's hard for anyone to overlook how the area has grown due to economic inclusion. When will other corporations, governments, individuals and groups learn that when pie is shared, there will be enough to go around because the pie will just keep getting bigger?

Also, as a black man, I have to speak of the need to educate, motivate and employ America's young black men. According to studies released in 2006 by specialists at Columbia, Princeton and Harvard, young African-American males have grown disconnected from society to a staggering degree. In 2004, half of all black men in their twenties were unemployed and 21 percent of black men who did not attend college were in prisons. The studies show the root of the trend is poor schooling. When I look back, my background should have placed me squarely on the road to being among those dismal statistics. Surely, I would have been a statistic if a few key people had not stepped in to keep me on the right path and, where necessary, help make a way where there may not have otherwise been a way. I've tried to do the same thing for others: fighting for the young in foster care, for non-violent low-level drug offenders, and against racial profiling. In light of the help afforded troubled black females through programs such as welfare, food stamps and public housing assistance, hopefully America will look at more ways to help young black men and discard its "lock the door and throw away the key" philosophy toward them. The economic costs of keeping them down are too high.

My humble start in the river bottoms of Lauderdale County, Tennessee, served as my springboard to become a pioneer in a number of areas. I was among the first blacks to serve as a quality control inspector for a major manufacturing company, the first to own and operate an aviation business in the city known as the "Air Capital of the World," one of the few black FAA inspectors, one of the early leaders in the government's 8A minority business program, the first to charter a minority bank in Wichita, the third person of color to serve on the Wichita City Council and one of a few African-Americans to serve in the Kansas Legislature. That my aviation business, Aero Services, became a leading distributor for one of the world's most acclaimed personal aircraft companies and a million-dollar operation shows what sheer determination can do. Had I been born wealthy or even middle-class I likely would not have worked so hard. Had I received more education or settled in a bigger city, I possibly would have achieved even greater success.

A closing thought: Because I retired as a state senator a year before the end of my term, a precinct committee from my county met to elect a person to complete my term. Whomever they selected would benefit by gaining the title of incumbent in a fall election field that was sure to be crowded. I hoped he or she would be a minority and motivated to try to make a difference, and I was pleased with the selection of Donald Betts, a twenty-seven-year-old African-American who was mid-way through

Following my retirement Donald Betts replaced me in the Kansas Senate in 2004.

his first term in the Kansas House of Representatives. He has maintained his Senate position as of 2006, but is still one of only two blacks in the chamber; the other, from Kansas City, is David Haley, the son of George Haley, the former state senator and ambassador to Gambia who played with me as a child on a dirt street in Tennessee.

Some things never change.

Spending part of my retirement relaxing in a way I couldn't before the 1960s. I possibly put a dozen balls in that water.

Appendix

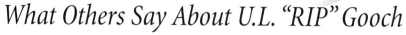

What Others Say About U.L. "RIP" Gooch

Franklin Rhodes, teacher

In all schools, you have people who misbehave. Rip was not in that class. He was an upper-class student in terms of how he conducted himself, never gave any trouble at all. Always ready to ask questions and answer the questions you ask him, and ready to put his hand forth to do any kind of thing. All the teachers thought well of him. He and his buddy [James Carthell Hayes] were mechanically minded.

Samuel Lee, friend

The fact of the matter is, we met in high school and he was 'Ulysses.' I had never met anyone who had that name. I found it quite fascinating because I had read Greek mythology, but I had never seen a person whose name was Ulysses. I began to look at some other aspects of him and found him to be a different individual.

When we came to high school, all the fellas would enroll in what we called agricultural programs, New Farmers of America. We had a lot of beautiful experiences with our ag teacher, who was also our principal. I found out that even though we were reciting these poems about the Country Boy's Creed – like 'I believe in the dignity of farm work and that I shall prosper ...' – that was not for Gooch! Gooch doesn't like farming, his friends told me. Every time a plane flies over, he has got his eyes set on the sky. He was in the class and he played his role. He was always an outgoing person and liked to be involved in things.

During this period, World War II was in progress and there was a lot of excitement about the war. Some of the fellas were volunteering to go to the war, and Gooch happened to be one of them. I had two very close friends who volunteered, and we were proud of them because these guys were brave and outgoing. I think Gooch saw an opportunity to fulfill one of his goals: he wanted to get around some airplanes. We didn't have any airplanes in Ripley!

We always had a good time at parties. Gooch managed to get things somehow that most of us couldn't get. He was always very resourceful.

Stan Wisdom, lawyer

I met Rip by coincidence. I started practicing law in July 1953 and one of the first pieces of business that came my way was incorporating the Bell Telephone Employees Flying Club. Fortunately, they couldn't afford an attorney and I couldn't afford to join them in their flying venture. I very quickly worked out an arrangement with my law firm in which I would incorporate the flying club and pay it out of my salary at the rate of $5 per month. The Bell Telephone club let me use their airplane at a cost of $2 per hour against the legal fee of $200. It was a good economic tradeoff for everyone, and I flew well over 100 hours.

When I was ready to start my flying lessons, my stepbrother arranged for a supervisor from Boeing to meet me at the airfield. It wasn't long before I arrived that this black fellow came along. We started a conversation, and I had an immediate liking for him. Rip taught me to fly that airplane and much more. We have logged hundreds of hours flying together all over the hemisphere.

A few years after Rip taught me to fly he expressed an interest in getting into the flying business for himself. We accomplished that. I was pleased to be his partner for many years in the aircraft business connected with a fixed-base operation at Wichita's Rawdon Field, Aero Services, which progressed to become the largest Mooney Aircraft distributorship in the United States. This spanned seventeen years and gave me an opportunity to get to know Rip on an intimate basis.

I have always been impressed with the fact that Rip's parents named him after the two commanding generals of the Civil War, an unusual thing to do in light of all the problems that confronted a black family in that time and area. Perhaps some of Rip's great moral depth and character stem from a family like that. It is in keeping with Rip's own view of life that he would simply refer to himself by a name that reflects his origin of Ripley, Tennessee. I have seen Rip in circumstances that would test the patience of any man. Some of those situations would bring tears to any feeling person's eyes. I marvel in the way he conducted himself as a man. He was always above and beyond those who would try to bring him down to their level.

If you were to ask me about Rip, I would simply say that I have never met a finer man in all my life. No man whom I would prefer to call "brother" has ever crossed my path.

Earl Chandler, banker

In 1960, I was a loan officer at the Union National Bank of Wichita and Rip was a customer there, and I'd heard about him because he was a black guy in a white guy's business. [Lawyer] Stan Wisdom was a good friend of mine whom Rip had taught to fly. Through that connection I became more interested than I would have been otherwise in what he was doing. We became friends long after I became his banker.

At that time Rip was struggling with Aero Services and the bank was struggling to keep him alive, and they dumped it on me. I was new to banking; I had been manager of a car dealership and worked at GMAC before that, so the bank put me in installment loans. I just felt like I was dealing with somebody that was really honest and really interesting but had no working capital, no money, and I didn't see how he was going to stick it out - but I didn't understand his business. He came in the bank one day, and said, "I need a banker that understands a fixed-base operation."

"Well, Rip," I said, "I've always been interested in aviation but I don't know anything about FBOs."

"Tell you what I'll do," Rip said, "I'll teach you to fly for nothing if you promise to learn about my business."

Like any guy who didn't have money but did have ambition, I jumped on that deal. We went through the instructing, but I didn't tell my wife because she'd have been worried sick.

At the time I had friends across the country who would call me up to tell me the latest racial joke; I was just a hidden redneck. I was hiding it from Rip, not wanting him to know what I was really like. I got to liking him so much, I thought he was an exception. He told me a lot of things as we were flying around the country. If he needed somebody to fly an airplane someplace, which often happened, I would follow him while he was delivering it or we'd go pick one up. He'd let me fly - free flying time for me. With Rip it was never, "Let's sit here and talk," it was always, "You've got to be learning something." He was such a great instructor, which I knew from Stan, but he was so much better than I thought he'd be. But I had to get used to instantly doing whatever a black person told me to do without thinking about it. He was very demanding, but I appreciated that.

After very few incidents, I realized this guy knew what he was doing and I liked him. We got to the point where I would question him about current-events issues, which in the 1960s equaled Civil Rights and race relations. There was a black congressman named Adam Clayton Powell whom I thought should be boxed up and put some place so he could never bother anyone again. Rip told me, "You know, Earl, what you'll find, I think, is that as people who are in the limelight like Powell or Martin Luther King, whoever replaces them will be far more controversial than they were." I've never forgotten that, and it proved to be true - Powell was one of the most moderate minorities we had in Congress.

I also found out about the terrible discrimination Rip had gone through, but he never complained about it, it was always, "I'm going to tell you a story," or just in talking that he mentioned it. I experienced several instances with him. We flew down to Kerrville, Texas, where the Mooney plant is, just the two of us, and it was lunchtime and he said we could go in the cafeteria to eat. I could see the panic in the eyes of the girl handing out the trays. She was probably 17 or 18 years old and didn't know whether to refuse service, run for help or just cry. She ended up running for help. The manager told her he knew Rip and it OK to serve us. The lesson for me was that I was furious, because it was me they weren't going to let eat with him. I felt like I was being discriminated against, and then I realized what he must feel like all the time.

One of the times he let me fly for nothing we went to a Mooney meeting at a lake resort in Austin, Texas. We flew in on the private landing strip and saw the golf course. I had brought my clubs, and though Rip didn't play at the time he said he'd go along for company. After nine holes, we stopped in the club house for some Cokes, and the guy in there said to me, "You can come in, but your caddy can't."

"He's not my caddy. He's hosting me here as a Mooney distributor," I told the man, but he would have none of that. Rip handled it well, but later the manager of the course came up and apologized to me and said he knew who Rip was. My point, though, was that it didn't matter who Rip was - if he was my caddy it would still have been a rotten thing to do. I told the manager we wouldn't be visiting the resort again.

Another time in Kerrville, at a Mooney distributor meeting with everyone from the United States and Canada, maybe the world, we were at a hotel where all the help was black - waiters, bus boys, etc. Stan Wisdom was with us, and I mentioned to him that I noticed we were getting treated better than anyone else there. "That's always the way it is with Rip at this kind of a deal," Stan said. All the help seemed to know Rip and would call him by name. He said, "You know, I don't really know that fella's name but he sure knows me; I wonder if it's because I'm the only black in 500 white people."

Ray Rowhuff, former pilot with Aero Services

To me, in aviation, I had two fathers. One was the guy who led me through flight school, Don O'Toole, and the guy who got me into the general aviation side, Rip Gooch. Nobody ever worked "for" Rip; you always worked "with" Rip - and he really believes that, it's not just lip service.

Rip always took care of his people. Like when I had a helicopter accident down in Enid, Oklahoma, he didn't tell anybody what happened. He sent someone down to pick me up, and called my wife and told her I'd be a little late so nobody would get excited, worried, concerned and all that. I thought Rip couldn't have handled that in any better fashion than the way he did it.

[Ray became a valuable asset to Aero Services, as well as its second-longest-lasting employee. By the time he started there, a large portion of the business' flight students and plane buyers were doctors and lawyers, and that would play an important role in Ray's future. Marvin Autry, a student of Ray's who later worked as an instructor at Aero Services, became friends with our client Dr. Dan Roberts, head of obstetrics and gynecology at Wesley Medical Center, and they formed the city's air ambulance service. When the service switched from planes to helicopters in the mid-1970s, Marvin hired Ray to set up the new program. Ray stayed with Marvin's company for two decades.]

Marvin Autry, head of fixed-base operation at Wichita's Jabara Airport

I came to Wichita in the last half of 1967 straight from Thailand, in the Air Force. I got stationed at Wichita's McConnell Air Force Base and started looking for a place to finish up my flight ratings. Someone recommended Aero Services.

I grew up in the mountains of North Carolina, in the South. That's important to be noted because growing up in the South, you very seldom see any black people having any kind of corporate jobs, specifically owning their own businesses. When I went out to Aero Services to enroll in flight training, I was shocked. I went in the Air Force right out of high school, so I had been in the military all my adult life, almost eight years, so I was shocked to see a black man who not only owned a business but was also a professional pilot - and an aircraft salesman. Rip was doing it all.

I started flight training with one of his instructors, Ray Rowhuff. They offered me a job as a lineman, servicing aircraft. When I would get off work from the Air Force, I'd come out and do line service for Rip. I obtained all my ratings and eventually went to work for him as a flight instructor. Leaving the Air Force and going to work for Rip was my first full-time job as an adult. While working for Rip and flight instructing, I eventually became his chief pilot. Though I left in 1971, I would return to occasionally fly for Rip when one of his other pilots was sick.

Rip's inspired me in a lot of ways, but I think one of the most positive things Rip ever did, I never have told him this, he gave me the confidence to go out on my own and start my own business, by example. I grew up in the South as a poor boy in the mountains, and I sat back, looked at Rip and said, "If a black guy can start a business in the 1950s and make it work, why can't a poor boy from North Carolina do the same thing?"

The operation at Wichita's Jabara Airport is a direct result of that. My fixed-base operation here has grown to about 100 employees. I often think about that, if I hadn't gone to work for Rip, where would I have ended up?

Judy Baker, former Aero Services secretary

When I went to work at Aero Services, they had the hangar where the guys work on the airplanes, and hangars for storage. During the time I worked there, because of the helicopter rotor hub contract, the pilots and instructions, and people renting planes it was a pretty active place. The customers were friendly, and the people who worked there were friendly.

My mother, Arlene Nelson, was Rip's secretary and ended up being his longest lasting employee. The business needed someone who could type contracts fast, and Mom called me to take a job doing that because she was not a fast typist. Rip would have to grab contracts as soon as they were done and head to Washington, D.C. One time the weather was freezing and the power went out, so I couldn't use the electric typewriter. While I used a manual one, Rip stood behind me with flashlight so I could see. Like Mom, I worked at Aero Services until it closed. I started doing payroll for him, and whatever needed to be done, kind of a Girl Friday.

While Mom worked with Rip, she learned to fly. It was so funny, my mother decided to get a private license and joined the American Women's Flying Association, and Dad said, "If you can do it, so can I." Then Mom went ahead and got her commercial license, but Dad never could get that done! She loved the book-keeping and the flying end of it; Rip would sometimes send her to deliver or pick up planes. She was pretty sharp, and sometimes she and Rip would go at it, they wouldn't agree on something and have a pretty good discussion - whatever it took to make the place run. He listened to Mom, he had a lot of respect for her. When Rip went out of business, Mom got a real estate license and sold for a company in Derby, Kansas.

Deryl Schuster, former Small Business Administration area manager

During the Lyndon Johnson administration, Secretary of War Robert McNamara identified a section of the Small Business Administration Act which in times of crisis permits the SBA to go directly to a small business and negotiate a procurement without having to go through the bidding process. That is Section 8A of the SBA Act. McNamara went to the president and said, "You know, we can use this to promote minority enterprise development."

The plan then languished until the Nixon administration, when the president said, "You will do this." We received an executive order. The government put pressure on the contracting officers around the country to identify contracts that could be given to minority firms qualified to do the work. Unfortunately there wasn't a government contracting officer in the country at the time who liked the program. They greatly disliked the program because it increased their workload. The contract Rip Gooch received, that we talked him into, I remember because it gave me gray hair - the helicopter rotor hub repairs that heretofore had been done by Bell Helicopter. Bell's contract was always a cost-plus: they were never locked into any price. However, the government made Rip do it on a fixed price. When you get into a rotor, you don't know what you're getting into - you may have to replace whatever, and Rip could lose money on the deal.

Now, Bell had a couple of machines paid for and built by the government that they used for the final testing of the overhauled rotor hubs. Bell owned the design, and the government would not give us one of these machines to let Rip use in his plant, so we had an SBA government procurement expert go to Bell Helicopter's plant and take photographs of this damn machine in a clandestine manner. From the photographs, Rip made one of these testing machines.

The SBA contracting officers made life miserable for Rip, though. They didn't like the program because they had to work. Back when the contract was with Bell Helicopter, they could sit around and drink coffee all day. There was a procurement office out of Denver that helped district SBA offices in the Midwest, and we received a lot of help from those guys trying to get reasonableness out of the government inspectors who tried to reject the hubs overhauled by Aero Services. In all the time that Rip was overhauling the helicopter rotor hubs that were coming from Vietnam and sending them back, there wasn't one single rejection in the field.

The trouble with the inspectors caused a of lot of governmental negotiation, during which time Rip was doing the job but starving to death, losing money. I've got to say I think that contract did him more economic harm than anything, but he produced magnificently. They tell me that the 8A Program today is a workable one, a good program creating minority entrepreneurs. Back then it probably hurt more people, except for the kitchen police-type projects [custodians, food service providers] - those were very successful and some guys made lots of money. But when you get into complicated, sophisticated manufacturing businesses, I'd bet the early days of the 8A Program hurt more minority entrepreneurs than it helped. It cost Rip Gooch dearly.

Walt Lesline, car dealer

I had taken flight lessons at Aero Services, but I didn't become very acquainted with Rip until I bought a plane from him in partnership with Glen Stearman and Dick Brown, who was the regional manager for the Dale Carnegie seminars.

I remember when Rip decided to get out of Aero Services and sell cars. Bob Herndon was my sales manager and I asked him to send Rip down to Associated Personnel Technicians and run a test on him to see if he'd be adaptable to selling cars. He's such a damn good friend I didn't want to hire him and then have to let him go. Rip took the test, and it said that he couldn't sell cars. But he kept calling us every three or four days. I finally told Bob Herndon, "I don't care what that test says, if Rip follows up on cars like he has with coming to work here, he's going to sell something."

The test was wrong. Rip sold a lot of cars. If I ever met a disgruntled customer of his, I don't know who it was - which is highly unusual. He was a hardworking salesman, which is also unusual. Most car salesmen want to know about 4:30 if you're going to close early. With Rip, I was there night after night until 10 o'clock after he had a late customer. In fact, it's strange how many people I still run into today who bought cars from Rip, even though I haven't had the dealership for sixteen years. I was up at Bed and Biscuit pet grooming recently, and I was wearing my Midwest Corporate Aviation hat, from when I kept my plane at Jabara Airport.

The lady asked me if I worked out at Midwest Corporate Aviation. I told her I kept my plane there when I owned a Buick store. "Well, do you know Rip Gooch? I bought my car from him in 1976," said the woman.

That's nothing unusual. I run into people all the time who want to know if I've talked to him, and he does likewise. We were real close, flew all over the United States together. After Rip came to work for me, I decided I wanted a little bigger airplane to carry people to car auctions. My Mooney was a very economical plane but it wasn't the roomiest plane. Rip and I bought a Beechcraft in 1985, built to our specifications. I let Rip oversee the deal because he knew more about airplanes. I told him, "Now, I understand you can request an end number [part of the plane's identification number, such as 123-AB], and it sure would be nice if we could get a triple number because they're easy to say - triple five, triple two, whatever. With 'WL' on the end of it for my initials, it would make a nice number."

You know what the number was? Triple six!

"Rip, damn it, that's the Devil's number," I said.

"Well, Walt, that was the only one available in WL."

I was well known when I went around the country; they'd remember me if I went there once - 666-WL.

I decided to get my instrument rating for the plane, and though former Aero Services instructor Charlie Seitz gave me my training, Rip was an examiner and I knew he'd be the one to examine me for my rating. One night, we were at the dealership working late, and I asked what I thought was an innocent question, "Rip, when you're taking your instrument check ride, are you allowed to use auto-pilot while you're looking over your charts?"

He was sitting in a swivel chair on the showroom floor and he got to laughing so hard he almost fell out of his seat. He assured me I couldn't use my auto-pilot while looking at charts; I was supposed to fly the plane and do that. He was a real good examiner. He'd forget he was working for me. I was working for him when we did that test.

Jo Brown, former Wichita School Board member

Rip had let himself be known to African-Americans, whites and various civic organizations, and he was a person who was likable and elect-able. Rip was his own best PR person. Rip was great, absolutely great. He couldn't always get his sentences going in the right direction, and I can be quoted on that and nobody will deny it. Sometimes he couldn't find out quite where to put the periods but he just kept on until he finally got his thought through.

He was "Johnny on the Job." You have to give credit where it's due, and there's no question that Rip was knowledgeable. He did his homework. He wasn't anybody who could be pushed around. Many people thought they were going to walk right over him, but he wasn't easy to walk over. He handled hidden agendas well. He was the kind of person who listened to Democrats and Republicans. It's mighty good to have a talking, working relationship with not only your friends but with your adversaries. And that was a key attribute of Rip's character. It's not easy. He knew how to work with people who did not have the same opinion that he had. He would listen to them and they'd listen to him. He was a good communicator with people who did not sit on the same side of the table as he did, so to speak.

Bob Knight, former mayor of Wichita

It was Rip's leadership that made a difference on the city council when he served. He was a courageous and honorable man who stood up for his convictions.

When people told us things couldn't be done repeatedly, we repeatedly did it and we did it almost every time by figuring out strategies and pulling together and trying to do the right thing and not just the political thing. Because a lot of what we did wasn't necessarily popular politically, but over a period of time as people see a work product they start to understand what they didn't understand before. They start understanding that well trained people are good for the community, that people that need a helping hand can come back and offer two helping hands to others and Rip had the wisdom to understand all of this.

J.C. Gilkey, district bishop for the Churches of God in Christ

As a visionary, Rip took the initiative and saw what could be done and what 21st Street could become. It was an eyesore; it was so disgusting to drive down 21st Street. If residents opposed him, he got stronger; he knew what was better for us and this community. I appreciated Rip because Rip wasn't thinking of himself per se. He dealt with those people against him and believed in his ideas. To drive down 21st Street now, people can say this is our community. Rip fought for the changes: better houses, getting streets repaired, beautifying the neighborhood. You had to have somebody to speak for you and speak for those who have needs. Rip was concerned about the little people who couldn't help themselves, didn't know how and didn't know who to turn to or go to. Rip was a go-to person.

Sherman Jones, former state senator

Being an African-American senator in the state of Kansas, you're a senator for all black folks it seemed. You're called upon from various people around the state to help, so Rip and I discussed this and he seemed OK about responding to folks not from Wichita.

I had served a couple of terms in House of Representatives before Rip came to

Topeka. We were Democrats and we were going up against Republicans. Rip was an experienced politician with experience on how to negotiate and debate. He was well polished in that area. We just didn't go into a debate or issue because we were different or happened to be black; we studied it first and decided who would cover the bill or who would not.

Marge Petty, former state senator

Rip and I were senators together and worked together eight years. We worked on juvenile justice issues – talking about young people getting charged for drugs. But Rip pointed out how we needed to look at the big picture, the money laundering that was going on. We needed to get to the source of the problem to help save those juveniles and it would benefit the Kansas community as a whole. He raised my level of understanding to such a greater degree.

When he first came in, I was to show him the ropes and mentor to him. In many ways he ended up mentoring me. I think he is amazing in terms of being a self-made man and what he's created in his life and accomplished, and also what he has given back. Rip in my opinion is as honest as they come. He is a real trailblazer, so to speak in more ways than one.

Besides his economic savvy, he was so perceptive of problems within the state bureaucracy or just within various communities. He'd be real quiet in the committee then make a comment that would cut to the heart of the issue. His wisdom in being able to cut to the chase and his ability to ask the hard questions were amazing.

One time when the Senate was thinking small, Rip passed out a poem and his message was to think bigger with some compassion. To me, the poem had a memorable last line, "Providing people enough wood to keep themselves warm." The poem served as a constant reminder to think bigger than the small debates we would get into.

Carolyn Wims-Campbell, the second secretary to Sen. Gooch

After Rip's secretary, Velda Duette, died and I replaced her, he said, "You know, Velda trained me." And I said, "Velda trained me, too," so we got a jumpstart on the ground rules for the secretarial position. I had worked with Velda several years before Sen. Gooch arrived. She had all kinds of connections, and she'd go outside to smoke and she'd find out things way before they were publicized. Sometimes Sen. Gooch would come in the office and say, "What are you hearing about such and such?" and I'd say I didn't hear anything because I didn't have that same connection and I wouldn't go outside to smoke. Velda was a Democrat from the heart – her father took her to union meetings when she was young. You could never find a more loyal, tough person; she didn't play. Many in the capitol received the blunt end of her.

I don't think Rip realized he made as big a difference in the Senate as he did; part of that was he became frustrated and unable to accomplish goals and things he wanted to change. Among his frustrations was a bill for individuals suffering from substance abuse; it really bothered him that [legislators] couldn't look at it as a way to help people improve the world instead of just locking them up. He'd say, "I'm sick and tired of being sick and tired," a famous quote from a speech made by activist Fannie Lou Hamer at the 1964 National Democratic Convention.

Rip was and continues to be concerned about the lack of diversity in the permanent employees in our state capitol building outside custodial positions. Each year we would attempt to identify the number and it has never been more than five or six. One day Sen. Gooch came into the office with a binder of the various commissions that are available for the governor to make appointments, and asked me to review them and identify ones that he might be able to make recommendations for African-Americans, especially those that provided stipends. He has never forgotten his brothers and sisters and is always attempting to find ways to empower them.

That last year, the 2003 legislative session, he was an energetic legislator; conscientious about his meetings and appointments; he reminded me of that song, "I Ain't No Way Tired." Some elected people aren't as truly concerned and dedicated as Rip; many come with their own personal agendas, not focused on making Kansas a better state. My father died when I was three, but Rip would just be the perfect replacement if I could have one.

Kathleen Sebelius, Governor of Kansas

Sen. Rip Gooch is a man of integrity, a role model and a leader. He has served the people of Wichita and Kansas in ways that can never be measured.

George Haley, former U.S. ambassador to Gambia and brother of author Alex Haley

As is told in this book, the life of Rip Gooch has been a combination of joys and sorrows, challenges, opportunities and successes. I am pleased to know Rip and to have remembered him as a child growing up in a little segregated country town in Western Tennessee. Rip's book reveals what the Heavenly Father can do with lives that sometimes seem so hopeless and desolate in early stages, making them very meaningful and highly significant to us all.

Acknowledgments

I would like to thank the people who have assisted in this book's writing and production:

Ed Andrews	Al Kamus
Marvin Autry	Bob Knight
Judy Baker	Samuel Lee
Don Benedict	J.V. Lentell
Wilma Black	Walt Lesline
George Boyd	Jay Nance
Josephine Brown	Larry Niebler
Earl Chandler	Charles Pearson
Bennie Clay	Marge Petty
Dan Close	Herb Rea
Jim Edwards	Franklin Rhodes
Gail Finney	Ray Rowhuff
J.C. Gilkey	Deryl Schuster
Bonita Gooch	Jerry Smartt
Camille Gooch	Ruby Stevens
George Haley	Ron Walters
George T. Johnson	Zenobia Washington
Robert Johnson	Carolyn Wims-Campbell
Sherman Jones	Stan Wisdom

I want to also acknowledge several people who have passed on since this project was started: Ted Davidson, John Halliburton, James Carthell Hayes and Tom Hemphill.

About the Authors

U.L. "Rip" Gooch is a pilot with 20,000 flight hours, a retired FAA pilot examiner and retired Kansas state senator, among other careers. A member of the Black Aviation Hall of Fame, he currently lives in Wichita, Kansas.

Glen Sharp is a Wichita-based freelance journalist who has served as a correspondent for The New York Times and Newsweek.